Graham Greene

TRAVELS WITH MY AUNT

Adapted by Giles Havergal

OBERON BOOKS
LONDON

First published in this adaptation in 1991 by Oberon Books Ltd
521 Caledonian Road, London N7 9RH
Tel: 020 7607 3637 / Fax: 020 7607 3629
e-mail: info@oberonbooks.com
www.oberonbooks.com

Reprinted in 2010

A catalogue record for this book is available from the British
Library.

ISBN: 978-1-87025-922-4

Cover Image by Shailahoti
Cover Design by Dan Stewart

Printed in Great Britain by CPI Antony Rowe Ltd, Chippenham

TRAVELS WITH MY AUNT

Characters

HENRY PULLING

AUNT AUGUSTA

WORDSWORTH

MISS KEENE

DETECTIVE SERGEANT SPARROW

HATTY

TOOLEY

O'TOOLE

MR VISCONTI

COLONEL HAKIM

TURKISH POLICEMAN

MISS PATERSON

RICHARD PULLING

VICAR

TAXI DRIVER

GIRL IN JODHPURS

POLICEMAN

ITALIAN GIRL

FRAU GENERAL SCHMIDT

WOLF

HOTEL RECEPTIONIST

SPANISH GENTLEMAN

BODYGUARD

YOLANDA

This adaptation can be staged with a large or a small cast and there are many schemes for doubling to suit the circumstances of the production and the wishes of the director.

Although the cast list numbers 24 (15M, 9F), the original production was presented with four actors only. Their parts are signified in the text by the numbers 1, 2, 3 and 4. Actors 1, 2 and 3 played Henry Pulling and divided the other parts between them. Actor 4 was silent except for two lines, but played a significant part in the action. The details of the original doubling are on the next page.

Many different locations are required, and this can be achieved in any way to suit the director. In the original production, we used a large digital display screen which flashed up the different locations. We also used music to help describe locations and as theme music for certain characters.

I would like to thank my colleagues in the original production at the Citizens' Theatre Glasgow, Christopher Gee, Patrick Hannaway and Derwent Watson who made up the cast, Jon Pope who directed the play with me and Stewart Laing who designed it.

CHARACTERS

Actor 1 played   Henry Pulling
                  Aunt Augusta

Actor 2 played   Henry Pulling
                  Tooley
                  O'Toole
                  Miss Keene
                  Frau General Schmidt
                  Italian Girl
                  Yolanda
                  Richard Pulling
                  Vicar
                  Policeman

Actor 3 played   Henry Pulling
                  Wordsworth
                  Mr Visconti
                  Colonel Hakim
                  Miss Paterson
                  Hatty
                  Detective Sergeant Sparrow
                  Spanish Gentleman
                  Taxi Driver

Actor 4 played   Henry Pulling
                  Girl in Jodhpurs
                  Wolf
                  Hotel Receptionist
                  Turkish Policeman (non-speaking)
                  Bodyguard (non-speaking)

Travels With My Aunt was first presented at the Citizens' Theatre, Glasgow on November 10th 1989. The production was directed by Giles Havergal and Jon Pope, designed by Stewart Laing with lighting designed by Gerry Jenkinson, with the following cast: Patrick Hannaway, Giles Havergal, Christopher Gee and Derwent Watson.

Act One

HENRY (1): I met my Aunt Augusta for the first time in more than half a century at my mother's funeral. My mother was approaching eighty-six when she died, and my aunt was some eleven or twelve years younger. I had retired from the bank two years before with an adequate pension and a silver handshake.

HENRY (2): Everyone thought me lucky but I found it difficult to occupy my time. I had never married. I had always lived quietly, and, apart from my interest in dahlias, I had no hobby. For those reasons I found myself agreeably excited by my mother's funeral.

HENRY (3): My father had been dead for more than forty years. He was a building contractor of a lethargic disposition who used to take afternoon naps in all sorts of curious places.

HENRY (1): As a child I remember going to the bathroom – we lived in Highgate then – and finding my father asleep in the bath in his clothes. I am rather short-sighted. I thought that my mother had been cleaning an overcoat, until I heard my father whisper

RICHARD PULLING (2). Bolt the door on the inside when you go out.

HENRY (1): He was too sleepy to realize that his order was quite impossible to carry out.

Crematorium organ music.

VICAR (2): A man that is born of woman hath but a short time to live and is full of misery.

HENRY (1): Not many people attended the crematorium, but there was that slight stirring of excited expectation which is never experienced at a graveside. Will the oven doors open? Will the coffin stick on the way to the flames?

HENRY (3): I heard a voice behind me –

AUNT AUGUSTA (1): I was present once at a premature cremation.

HENRY (3): Hush.

VICAR (2): In the name of the Father, Son and Holy Ghost.

ALL: Amen.

Organ music stops – Graveyard – birdsong.

HENRY (3): The funeral went without a hitch.

HENRY (2): Afterwards in the troubled sunlight I shook hands with a number of nephews and nieces and cousins whom I could not identify.

HENRY (1): It was understood that I had to wait for the ashes and wait I did.

HENRY (2): While the chimney of the crematorium gently smoked overhead.

AUNT AUGUSTA (1): You must be Henry.

HENRY (2): I recognized with some difficulty my Aunt Augusta dressed rather as the late Queen Mary of beloved memory might have dressed.

HENRY (3): I was surprised by her brilliant red hair. Yes, and you must be Aunt Augusta.

AUNT AUGUSTA (1): It's a very long time since I saw anything of your mother. I hope that her death was an easy one.

HENRY (3): Oh yes, you know, she was eighty-six – her heart just stopped. She died of old age.

AUNT AUGUSTA (1): Old age? She was only twelve years older than I am.

HENRY (1): Aunt Augusta said accusingly.

AUNT AUGUSTA (1): Tell me, are you still at the bank?

HENRY (3): No, I retired two years ago.

AUNT AUGUSTA (1): Retired? Why you can only be – let me see, fifty-five. For heaven's sake, what do you do with your time?

HENRY (3): I cultivate dahlias, Aunt Augusta.

AUNT AUGUSTA (1): Dahlias! Whatever would your father have said!

HENRY (3): He took no interest in flowers. He always thought a garden was a waste of good building space. He would calculate how many bedrooms one above the other he could have fitted in. He was a very sleepy man.

AUNT AUGUSTA (1): He needed bedrooms for more than sleep.

HENRY (1): My aunt said with a coarseness which surprised me.

HENRY (3): He slept in the oddest places. I remember once in the bathroom...

AUNT AUGUSTA (1): In a bedroom he did other things than sleep. You are the proof.

HENRY (1): I began to understand why my parents had seen so little of Aunt Augusta. She had a temperament my mother would not have liked.

HENRY receives the wrapped package containing urn.

AUNT AUGUSTA (1): What are you going to do with the ashes?

HENRY (3): I thought of making a little place for the urn among my dahlias.

AUNT AUGUSTA (1): It will look a little bleak in winter.

HENRY (3): Well, Aunt Augusta, it's been many years since we saw each other… I had left the lawn-mower outside, uncovered, and there was a hint of rain…. I would like it very much if one day you would take a cup of tea with me in Southwood.

AUNT AUGUSTA (1): At the moment I would prefer something stronger and more tranquillizing. It is not every day one sees a sister consigned to the flames. Like Joan the Maid.

HENRY (3): I don't quite…

AUNT AUGUSTA (1): Joan of Arc.

HENRY (3): I have some sherry at home, but it's rather a long ride.

AUNT AUGUSTA (1): My apartment is at any rate north of the river, and I have everything we require. Taxi!

SIGN – TAXI

Taxi sounds. In the taxi –

It's odd how we seem to meet only at religious ceremonies. The last time I saw you was at your baptism. I was not asked but I came. Like the wicked fairy!

HENRY (2): I didn't know there was any breach. Your photograph was there in the family album.

AUNT AUGUSTA (1): For appearances only. Your mother was a very saintly woman. She should by rights have had a white funeral.

HENRY (2): I don't quite see… a white funeral means… well, to put it bluntly, I am here, Aunt Augusta.

AUNT AUGUSTA (1): Yes. But you were your father's child. Not your mother's.

HENRY (1): My aunt answered casually.

HENRY (2): Hiccups are said to be cured by a sudden shock and they can equally be caused by one.

AUNT AUGUSTA (1): (*Henry hiccups though this.*) I have said that your official mother was a saint. The girl, you see, refused to marry your father. So my sister covered up for her by marrying him. My sister – your stepmother – perhaps we should agree to call her – was a very noble person indeed.

HENRY (2): And my – hic – father?

AUNT AUGUSTA (1): A bit of a hound, but so are most men. Perhaps it's their best quality. I hope you have a little bit of the hound in you too, Henry.

HENRY (2): I don't – hic – think so.

AUNT AUGUSTA (1): We may discover it in time. You are your father's son.

HENRY (2): Who was my mother? I asked. But my aunt was already speaking to the driver.

AUNT AUGUSTA (1): No, no, my man. This is the Crescent.

TAXI DRIVER (3): You said turn right, lady.

AUNT AUGUSTA (1): Then I apologize. I am always a little uncertain about right and left. Port I can always remember because of the colour – red means left. You should have turned to port not starboard.

TAXI DRIVER (3): I'm no bloody navigator, lady.

AUNT AUGUSTA (1): Never mind. Just continue all the way round and start again.

TAXI DRIVER (3): (*Taxi stops.*) Ma'am, if you had only told me it was the Crown and Anchor…

AUNT AUGUSTA (1): Henry, if you could forget your hiccups for a moment.

TAXI DRIVER (3): It's six and six on the clock.

AUNT AUGUSTA (1): Then we will let it reach seven shillings. Henry, I feel I ought to warn you that a white funeral in my case would have been quite out of place.

HENRY (2): But you've never been married... I said, very quickly to beat the hiccups...

AUNT AUGUSTA (1): I have nearly always, during the last sixty or more years, had a friend. Age, Henry, may a little modify our emotions – it does not destroy them.

SIGN – THE CROWN & ANCHOR

Saloon bar noises.

HENRY (1): Through the windows of the Crown and Anchor I could see men with exaggerated moustaches in tweed coats, which were split horsily behind, gathered round a girl in jodhpurs. They were not the type to whom I would have extended much credit.

HENRY (3): We went in by a side door. My aunt's apartment was on the second floor.

HENRY (2): Aren't you disturbed by the noise from the bar, I asked.

AUNT AUGUSTA (1): Oh no. And the bar is very convenient if I suddenly run short. I just send Wordsworth down.

HENRY (2): Who is Wordsworth?

AUNT AUGUSTA (1): I call him Wordsworth because I can't bring myself to call him Zachary.

HENRY (2): He's your valet?

AUNT AUGUSTA (1): Let us say he attends to my wants. A very gentle sweet strong person. But don't let him ask you for a CTC. He receives quite enough from me.

HENRY (2): What is a CTC?

AUNT AUGUSTA (1): That was what they called any tip or gift in Sierra Leone when he was a boy. The initials belonged to Cape to Cairo Cigarettes which all the sailors handed out generously.

HENRY (2): My aunt's conversation went too quickly for my understanding so that I was not really prepared for the very large middle-aged negro who opened the door.

SIGN – THE FLAT

Venetian Glass.

AUNT AUGUSTA (1): Why, Wordsworth, you've been washing up breakfast without waiting for me. This is my nephew, Wordsworth.

WORDSWORTH (3): You be telling me the whole truth, woman?

AUNT AUGUSTA (1): Of course I am. Oh, Wordsworth, Wordsworth!

HENRY (2): The lights were on in the living-room, and my eyes were dazzled for a moment by rays from the glass ornaments which flashed back from every open space.

AUNT AUGUSTA (1): Wordsworth, be a dear and fetch us two whiskies. Augusta feels a teeny bit sad after the sad sad ceremony.

HENRY (1): She spoke to him as though he were a child – or a lover, but that relationship I was reluctant to accept.

WORDSWORTH (3): Everything go OK? No bad medicine?

AUNT AUGUSTA (1): There was no contretemps. Oh gracious, Henry, you haven't forgotten your parcel?

HENRY (2): No, no, I have it here.

AUNT AUGUSTA (1): I think perhaps Wordsworth had better put it in the refrigerator.

HENRY (2): Quite unnecessary, Aunt Augusta.

AUNT AUGUSTA (1): Let Wordsworth put it in the kitchen. We don't want to be reminded all the time of my poor sister. I am especially attached to Venice because I began my real career there, and my travels. I have always been very fond of travel. It's a great grief to me that my travels now are curtailed.

HENRY (2): Age strikes us all before we know it.

AUNT AUGUSTA (1): Age? I was not referring to age. I hope I don't look all that decrepit, Henry, but I like having a companion and Wordsworth is very occupied now because he's studying to enter the London School of Economics.

WORDSWORTH brings whiskies.

I can say now to both of you how relieved I am that everything this afternoon went without a hitch. I once attended a very important funeral – the wife of a famous man of letters who had not been the most faithful of husbands. It was soon after the first great war. I was very interested at that time in the Fabians. I arrived early as a spectator and I was leaning over the Communion rail – trying to make out the names on the wreaths – and I must have accidentally touched a button. The coffin began to slide away, the doors opened, I could feel the hot air of the oven and hear the flap of the flames, the coffin went in and the doors closed, and at that very moment in walked the whole grand party. Mr and Mrs Bernard Shaw, Mr H G Wells, Doctor Havelock Ellis, Mr Ramsay MacDonald, and the widower. The clergyman (non-denominational of course) led us in the humanist hymn 'Cosmos, O Cosmos, Cosmos shall we call Thee?' I buried my face in my handkerchief and simulated grief, but you know I don't think anyone (except, I suppose, the clergyman and he kept dumb about it) noticed that the coffin wasn't there. The widower certainly didn't, but then he hadn't noticed his wife for some years. Doctor Havelock Ellis made a very moving address (or so it seemed to me then; I hadn't finally plumped for Catholicism, though I was on the brink) about the dignity of a funeral service conducted without illusions or rhetoric. He could truthfully have said without a corpse too.

WORDSWORTH (3): We must allays go careful careful at a funeral.

HENRY (2): I really think I must be going now, Aunt Augusta. I can't keep my mind off the mowing-machine. It will be quite rusted in this rain. It has made me so happy meeting you. You are my only close relative now.

AUNT AUGUSTA (1): As far as you know. Your father had spells of activity.

HENRY (2): My poor stepmother... I shall never be able to think of anyone else as my mother

AUNT AUGUSTA (1): Better so.

HENRY (2): You will come one day and see my dahlias, won't you? They are in full bloom.

AUNT AUGUSTA (1): Of course, Henry. Do you enjoy travel?

HENRY (2): I've never had the opportunity.

AUNT AUGUSTA (1): With Wordsworth so occupied we might take a little trip or two together.

HENRY (2): Gladly, Aunt Augusta. It never occurred to me that she meant further than the seaside.

HENRY (1): Wordsworth showed me to the door and as I pushed past the window of the Crown and Anchor I heard the girl in the jodhpurs say –

GIRL IN JODHPURS (4): Peter can talk about nothing but cricket. All the summer it went on. Nothing but the fucking Ashes.

HENRY (1): I don't like to hear such adjectives on the lips of an attractive young girl, but her words reminded me sharply that I had left all that remained of my mother in Aunt Augusta's kitchen.

Rings bell – sound of intercom buzzer.

WORDSWORTH (3): Who be there?

HENRY (1): It's Henry Pulling.

WORDSWORTH (3): Don know anyone called that name.

HENRY (1): I've only just left you. I'm Aunt Augusta's nephew.

WORDSWORTH (3): Oh, that guy.

HENRY (1): I left a parcel with you in the kitchen.

WORDSWORTH (3): You wan it back?

HENRY (1): Please, if it's not too much trouble…

WORDSWORTH (3): It's a bloody lot of trouble. Stay there.

WORDSWORTH delivers urn – the wrapping paper is open.

HENRY (1): Thank you for the great trouble you have taken. Has somebody opened this?

WORDSWORTH (3): Ar just wan to see what you got there?

HENRY (1): You might have asked me.

WORDSWORTH (3): Why, man, you not offended at Wordsworth?

HENRY (1): Are you really studying for the London School of Economics?

WORDSWORTH (3): Oh, tha's a joke your auntie makes. Ar was workin at the Grenada Palace Cinema in Tooting. Ar had a uniform. Just lak a general. She lak ma uniform. She stop an say, 'Are you the Emperor Jones?' 'No, ma'am,' I say, 'arm only old Wordsworth.' 'Oh,' she say, 'thou child of joy, shout round me, let me hear thy shouts, thou happy shepherd boy.' 'You write that down for me,' ar say. 'It sound good, ar like it.'

HENRY (1): Well, Wordsworth, thank you for all your trouble.

WORDSWORTH (3): This here mighty important parcel?

HENRY (1): Yes. I suppose it is.

WORDSWORTH (3): Then ar think you owe a CTC to old Wordsworth.

HENRY (1): Remembering what my aunt had told me, I went quickly away.

SIGN – BACK HOME – SOUTHWOOD

My new lawn-mower was wet all over. I dried it carefully and oiled the blades. Then I boiled myself two eggs and made a cup of tea for lunch.

HENRY (3): I had much to think about. Could I accept my aunt's story and in that case who was my mother? And if indeed she had been only a step-mother did I still want to place her ashes among my dahlias?

SIGN – MISS KEENE

HENRY (2): (*Picks up letter.*) I recognized the handwriting of Barbara Keene. Her father, Sir Alfred Keene, had made a fortune in cement and had been one of the main depositors at the bank. Barbara was interested in tatting which she gave to the church bazaar. My mother had suggested that I might pay her attentions for she would certainly inherit Sir Alfred's money – but the motive seemed to me dishonest. The bank was my whole life and now there were my dahlias.

HENRY (3): Shortly before Sir Alfred had died and Miss Keene went to live in South Africa, on her last night in England she has asked me to dinner.

Coffee pot and cups.

MISS KEENE (2): I have sold the house as it stands with all the furniture.

HENRY (2): Said Miss Keene.

MISS KEENE (2): I shall live with second cousins.

HENRY (1): Do you know them well, I replied?

MISS KEENE (2): I have never seen them. We have only exchanged letters. Do you know South Africa?

HENRY (1): I have seldom been out of England.

MISS KEENE (2): My father was a very overwhelming personality. I never had friends – except you, of course, Mr Pulling. I shall be living near Koffiefontein.

HENRY (1): Where is that?

MISS KEENE (2): I don't really know.

HENRY (1): It seems a very long way to go.

MISS KEENE (2): If there was anything to keep me here… Will you take one lump or two?

HENRY (1): No sugar, thank you. It is astonishing how nearly I came to proposing marriage that night and yet I refrained. Our interests were different, of course – tatting and dahlias have nothing in common.

HENRY (3): Now she wrote.

MISS KEENE (2): Dear Mr Pulling, I wonder how Southwood is and whether it is raining. We are having a beautiful sunny winter. My cousins have a small farm of ten thousand acres and they think nothing of driving seven hundred miles to buy a ram. I am not quite used to things yet and I think often of Southwood. How are the dahlias? I have given up tatting.

Telephone rings.

AUNT AUGUSTA (1): You are very slow to answer. I have an extraordinary story to tell you. I have been raided by the police.

HENRY (2): Raided…? By the police ?

AUNT AUGUSTA (1): Yes, you must listen carefully for they may call on you.

HENRY (2): But Aunt Augusta… what happened?

AUNT AUGUSTA (1): It was midnight and Wordsworth and I had gone to bed. Luckily I was wearing my best nightdress. They rang the bell down below and told us through the microphone that they were police officers. They were rather surprised by Wordsworth – or perhaps it was the colour of his pyjamas. They said, 'Is this your husband, ma'am?' I said, 'No, this is Wordsworth.' The name seemed to ring a bell with one of them. They said they had reliable information that drugs were kept on the premises.

HENRY (2): WHAT!

AUNT AUGUSTA (1): They made a very thorough search, especially in Wordsworth's room. They even read some letters of mine and asked who Abdul was.

HENRY (2): Who was Abdul?

AUNT AUGUSTA (1): Someone I knew in Istanbul a very long time ago.

HENRY (2): I am sorry, Aunt Augusta. It must have been a terrifying experience.

AUNT AUGUSTA (1): It was amusing in a way. But it did give me a guilty feeling…

Bell rings.

HENRY (2): Hold on a moment, Aunt Augusta. Your friends, the police, are here, I'll ring you back when they've gone.

SPARROW (3): Mr Pulling?

HENRY (2): Yes.

SPARROW (3): May we come in for a few moments?

HENRY (2): Have you a warrant?

SPARROW (3): Oh, no, no, it hasn't come to that. We just want to have a word or two with you.

HENRY (1): I wanted to say something about the Gestapo, but thought it wiser not.

SPARROW (3): You know a man called Wordsworth, Mr Pulling?

HENRY (2): Yes, he's a friend of my aunt's.

SPARROW (3): Did you receive a package from him in the street yesterday?

HENRY (2): I certainly did.

SPARROW (3): Would you have any objection to our examining the package, Mr Pulling?

HENRY (2): I most certainly would. The package contained an urn with my mother's ashes.

SPARROW (3): And so those ashes... they are Mrs Pulling's?

HENRY (2): There they are. You can see for yourself. On the bookcase.

HENRY (1): I had put the urn there temporarily, above a complete set of Sir Walter Scott which I had inherited from my father. In his lazy way, he had been a great reader, though not an adventurous one. By the time he had read the set of Scott through he had forgotten the earlier volumes and was content to begin again with Guy Mannering. He had a love of nineteenth-century poetry which I had inherited – Tennyson and Wordsworth and Palgrave's Golden Treasury.

SPARROW (3): I would like to take a sample for analysis.

HENRY (2): If you think I am going to let you play around with my poor mother in a police laboratory...

SPARROW (3): I can understand how you feel, sir, but we have rather serious evidence to go on. We took some fluff from the man Wordsworth's pockets and when analyzed it contained pot.

HENRY (2): Pot?

SPARROW (3): Marijuana to you, sir. Likewise cannabis.

HENRY (2). Wordsworth's fluff has got nothing to do with my mother.

SPARROW (3): But you see, sir, it's quite possible that the man Wordsworth took out the ashes and substituted pot. He may have known he was being watched. Your aunt told us you planned to keep it in your garden – you wouldn't want to see that urn every day and wonder, are those really the ashes of the dear departed or are they an illegal supply of marijuana? We'd only take out a tiny pinch, sir.

HENRY (2): All right, take your pinch. I suppose you are only doing your duty. (*On telephone.*) They've taken away the urn. They think my mother's ashes are marijuana. Where's Wordsworth?

AUNT AUGUSTA (1): He went out after breakfast and hasn't come back.

HENRY (2): They found marijuana dust in the fluff of his suit.

AUNT AUGUSTA (1): Oh dear, how careless of the poor boy. I thought he was a little disturbed. And he asked for a CTC before he went out.

HENRY (2): Did you give him one?

AUNT AUGUSTA (1): I gave him twenty pounds.

HENRY (2): Twenty pounds! I never keep as much as that in the house.

AUNT AUGUSTA (1): It will get him as far as Paris. He left in time for the Golden Arrow, now I come to think of it. Do you know, Henry, I've a great desire for a little sea air myself.

HENRY (2): You'll never find him in Paris.

AUNT AUGUSTA (1): I wasn't thinking of Paris. I was thinking of Istanbul.

HENRY (2): I don't think I could manage Istanbul, Aunt Augusta, but I have nothing particular to do tomorrow. Perhaps you would like to take the sea air at Brighton…

AUNT AUGUSTA (1): (*Enthusiastically.*) Brighton!

SIGN – BRIGHTON

HENRY (2): I had booked rooms at the Royal Albion because my aunt wished to be near the Palace Pier.

AUNT AUGUSTA (1): I like to be at the centre of all the devilry, with the buses going off to all those places.

HENRY (3): She spoke as though their destinations were Sodom and Gomorrah rather than Lewes and Littlehampton. Apparently she had come first to Brighton when she was quite a young woman, full of expectations which were partly fulfilled.

AUNT AUGUSTA (1): We don't want dinner for another two hours. Now, we have to find Hatty.

HENRY (2): Who is Hatty?

AUNT AUGUSTA (1): We worked together once with a gentleman called Mr Curran.

HENRY (2): How long ago was that?

AUNT AUGUSTA (1): Forty years or more.

HENRY (2): It was a grey leaden evening with an east wind blowing sea sands. The sea was rising and the pebbles turned and ground under the receding waves.

HENRY (2): As we walked my aunt said a little sadly –

AUNT AUGUSTA (1): I wonder where Wordsworth is now.

HENRY (2): I expect you'll hear from him soon.

AUNT AUGUSTA (1): I very much doubt it, my dear Henry. At my age one has ceased to expect a relationship to last. I was very fond of Wordsworth but my emotions are not as strong as they once were. I can support his absence, though I may regret him for a while tonight. His knackers were superb.

HENRY (2): I was too surprised by her vulgarity to speak.

SIGN – HATTY'S TEAPOT – FORTUNES TOLD

AUNT AUGUSTA (1): Ah, it is here. Hatty's Teapot – Fortunes told by Appointment Only.

HENRY (1): We rang the bell and an old lady answered. She was wearing a black evening dress and a lot of jet objects jangled when she moved.

HATTY (3): You're too late.

AUNT AUGUSTA (1): Hatty.

HATTY (3): I close at six-thirty sharp except by special appointment.

AUNT AUGUSTA (1). Hatty, it's Augusta.

HATTY (3): Augusta?

AUNT AUGUSTA (1): Augusta Bertram.

HATTY (3): Augusta!

AUNT AUGUSTA (1): Hatty! You haven't changed a bit.

HATTY (3): It must be –

AUNT AUGUSTA (1): – forty years. This is my nephew Henry, Hatty. You remember about him.

HENRY (2): They exchanged a look which I found disturbing. Why should I have been discussed all those years ago? Had she let Hatty into the secret of my birth?

HATTY (3): Come on in, the two of you. I was just going to have a cup of tea – an unprofessional cup of tea.

Circus music.

SIGN – MR CURRAN

Mr Curran.

AUNT AUGUSTA (1): The Revered. Mr Curran.

HATTY (3): The circus, the elephant, the performing dogs – do you remember, Augusta?

AUNT AUGUSTA (1): Indeed I do. And the creation of The Doggies Church.

SIGN – THE DOGGIES CHURCH

I happened to be there when the elephant trod on Curran's toe, and we became very close friends. Poor man, he had to go to hospital, and while he was there two of the performing dogs came to see him.

HATTY (3): It was visiting day and there were a lot of women around to see their husbands.

AUNT AUGUSTA (1): At first the dogs weren't allowed into the ward but Mr Curran got round matron, telling her they weren't ordinary dogs, they were human dogs. They came up to the bed, wearing their pointed hats and pierrot collars, and each gave Curran a paw to shake and touched his face with its nose like an eskimo.

HATTY (3): You should have heard those women. 'The darlings, the sweet little doggies. Just like humans.' One woman asked, 'Are they gentleman doggies or lady doggies' as though she had been too refined to look. 'One of each,' Currain said, and just out of devilry he added, 'they were married a month ago. At the Doggies Church in Potters Bar.' 'Married in church?' they squealed and I really thought he'd gone too far, but how they swallowed it down.

AUNT AUGUSTA (1): You've started something, I said. And 'Why not?' Curran said, and The Doggies Church was created. I was a Deaconess.

HATTY (3): We made a fortune, for a while. We had all the dog-owners of Brighton and Hove behind us – they even came over from as far as Hastings. The police tried to get us once under the Blasphemy Act, but nobody could find any blasphemy in our services. They were very solemn.

AUNT AUGUSTA (1): Curran wanted to start the churching of bitches after the puppies came, but I said that was going too far. Then there was the question of marrying divorced couples – I thought it would treble our income, but Curran stood firm. 'We don't recognize divorce,' he said, and he was quite right – it would have sullied the sentiment.

HATTY (3): Then the police interfered.

AUNT AUGUSTA (1): They always do. They had him up for speaking to girls on the front, and a lot was said in court that wasn't apropos. I was young and angry and uncomprehending, and I wouldn't help him any more. No wonder he abandoned me. No one can stand not being forgiven. That's God's privilege.

HATTY (3): Would you like me to do a professional cup, dear, for you and your friend?

AUNT AUGUSTA (1): Nephew. It would be fun, dear.

HATTY (3): Now toss the tea away, dear, in this basin. It's interesting, very interesting. You are going to do a lot of travelling. With another person. You are going to have many adventures.

AUNT AUGUSTA (1): With men?

HATTY (3): That the leaves don't say, dear, but knowing you as I do, it wouldn't surprise me. You will be in danger of your life on more than one occasion.

AUNT AUGUSTA (1): But I'll come through?

HATTY (3): I see a knife – or it might be a syringe.

AUNT AUGUSTA (1): Or it could be something else, Hatty – you know what I mean?

HATTY (3): I see a lot of confusion – a lot of running about. I'm sorry, Augusta, but I can't see any peace at the end. There's a cross. Perhaps it's a double cross?

AUNT AUGUSTA (1): But you'll take one look at Henry's cup too, dear, won't you?

HATTY (3): Men are difficult. They have so many occupations beyond a woman's knowledge. Are you an undertaker?

HENRY (2): No.

HATTY (3): There's something that looks like an urn. Do you see it there?

HENRY (2): It might be an urn.

HATTY (3): You will do a lot of travelling with a lady friend.

HENRY (2): That's not very likely. I've always been rather stay-at-home. It's quite an adventure for me coming as far as Brighton.

HATTY (3): The leaves don't lie.

SIGN – SOUTHWOOD

HENRY (2): My aunt came to dinner with me later that week and announced –

AUNT AUGUSTA (1): I have booked two couchettes on the Orient Express.

HENRY (3): Where to?

AUNT AUGUSTA (1): Istanbul, of course.

HENRY (3): Why Istanbul?

AUNT AUGUSTA (1): Such a strange coincidence this morning. I had a letter in the post from Abdul – the first for a very long time.

HENRY (3): From Abdul?

AUNT AUGUSTA (1): Yes. He is asking me to invest in a new project in Turkey. The returns on the investment are very generous indeed.

HENRY (3): If you want to go to Istanbul surely it would be easier and less expensive to fly?

AUNT AUGUSTA (1): It is a matter of choice. I knew Wilbur Wright very well indeed at one time. He took me for several trips. I always felt quite secure in his contraptions. But I cannot bear being spoken to all the time by irrelevant loud-speakers.

HENRY (3): I'm sorry, Aunt Augusta, but a bank manager's pension is not a generous one.

AUNT AUGUSTA (1): I shall naturally pay all expenses.

HENRY (3): I'm not really accustomed to foreign travel.

AUNT AUGUSTA (1): You will take to it quickly enough in my company. The Pullings have all been great travellers. I think I must have caught the infection through your father.

HENRY (3): Surely not my father... He never travelled further than Central London.

AUNT AUGUSTA (1): He travelled from one woman to another, Henry. All through his life. That comes to much the same thing.

HENRY (3): But how are we going to manage on our Tourist Allowance? With fifty pounds each we shall not be able to stay very long in Istanbul.

AUNT AUGUSTA (1): I only intend to stay one day. Currency restrictions have never seriously bothered me. There are ways and means.

HENRY (3): I hope you don't plan anything illegal.

AUNT AUGUSTA (1): I have never planned anything illegal in my life. How could I when I have never read any of the laws and have no idea what they are?

HENRY (3): It was my aunt who suggested that we should fly as far as Paris. I was a little surprised at what she said. I pointed out the inconsistencies.

AUNT AUGUSTA (1): There are reasons, cogent reasons. I know the ropes at Heathrow.

SIGN – PARIS

HENRY (1): I had no clear idea what my aunt intended. There was obviously little danger from the douanier who waved us and our suitcases through with the careless courtesy which I find so lacking in the supercilious young men in England.

SIGN – THE ST JAMES HOTEL, PARIS

HENRY (2): My aunt had booked rooms in the St James Hotel.

HENRY (3): She had taken a whole suite, which seemed rather unnecessary as we were only spending one night before we caught the Orient Express.

HENRY (1): When I mentioned this, however, she rebuked me quite sharply.

AUNT AUGUSTA (1): This is the second time today that you have mentioned the subject of economy. You retain the spirit of a bank manager, even in retirement. Understand once and for all that I am not interested in economy. I am over seventy-five and my money is my own and I do not intend to save for the sake of an heir. In any case this suite is not wasted. I have to receive some visitors in private. One of them, by the way, is a bank manager.

HENRY (2): The man who came to see her was not my idea of a bank manager at all.

HENRY (3): He was tall and elegant with black side-burns and he would have fitted very well into a matador's uniform. My aunt asked me to bring her suitcase, and I then left them alone, but looking back from the doorway I saw that the lid was already open and the case seemed to be stacked with ten pound notes.

HENRY (2): I sat down in my bedroom and read a copy of Punch to reassure myself. The sight of all the smuggled money had been a shock. If the ten pound notes, I thought, were tied in bundles of twenty, there could easily be as much as three thousand pounds in the suitcase, or even six.

HENRY (3): Then I remembered the case was an expandable Revelation. Twelve thousand was not an impossible total. I felt a little comforted by that idea. Smuggling on such a large scale seemed more like a business coup than a crime.

SIGN – PARIS STREET

HENRY (1): I went restlessly out and walked up to the Place Vendome. Suddenly I saw bearing down on me with a happy grin of welcome, a man whom I recognized with apprehension.

WORDSWORTH (3): Mr Pullen?

HENRY (1): Wordsworth!

WORDSWORTH (3): Wot you doing here?

HENRY (1): I was just taking a little stroll.

WORDSWORTH (3): If you wan a girl you come along with Wordsworth.

HENRY (1): But I don't want a girl, Wordsworth. I am here with my aunt.

WORDSWORTH (3): Your auntie here? Praise to the holiest in the height.

HENRY (1): Yes. Tomorrow we take the Orient Express to Istanbul.

WORDSWORTH (3): Istanbul. What she do there? Who she go for see?

HENRY (1): I imagine we shall see the Blue Mosque, Santa Sophia, the Topkapi Museum...

WORDSWORTH (3): You be careful, Mr Pullen. You got CTC for me? Ar find you lovely gel, school-teacher.

HENRY (1): I don't want a school-teacher, Wordsworth. I gave him a ten-franc note to keep him quiet.

SIGN – BACK AT THE HOTEL

HENRY (2): I saw Wordsworth just now.

AUNT AUGUSTA (1): What? Here?

HENRY (2): I am sorry to disappoint you, no. Not here in the hotel. In the street.

AUNT AUGUSTA (1): Where is he living?

HENRY (2): I didn't ask. Nor did I give him your address. I hadn't realized that you would be so anxious to see him again.

AUNT AUGUSTA (1): You are a hard man, Henry.

HENRY (2): Not hard, Aunt Augusta. Prudent.

AUNT AUGUSTA (1): I don't know from which side of the family you inherited prudence. Your father was lazy but never, never prudent.

HENRY (2): And my mother?

AUNT AUGUSTA (1): If she had been prudent you would not be here now.

HENRY (2): Would you have liked a child, Aunt Augusta?

AUNT AUGUSTA (1): At most times it would have been inconvenient. Curran was not to be trusted as a father and by the time I knew Mr Visconti the hour was really getting late. In any case I would have made a very unsatisfactory mother. And suppose the child had turned out completely respectable...

HENRY (2): Like myself?

AUNT AUGUSTA (1): I don't yet despair of you, Henry.

HENRY (2): Who was Mr Visconti?

AUNT AUGUSTA (1): Ah! Mr Visconti! We first met here in Paris at the 'Exhibition' in the Rue Pigalle.

HENRY (2): 'Exhibition'? Exhibition of what?

AUNT AUGUSTA (1): Mr Visconti said I had a fine talent, and he persuaded me to leave the girls I was performing with and travel with him to Italy where my career really started.

SIGN – GARE DE LYON

Station noises, steam.

HENRY (1): That night at the Gare de Lyon I saw my aunt into her couchette and waited for a few moments on the platform.

WORDSWORTH (3): Hi, fellah.

HENRY (1): What are you doing here, Wordsworth?

WORDSWORTH (3): Ar allays was your friend, Mr Pullen. You no humbug me, Mr Pullen? Where's that gel?

HENRY (1): My aunt, if that's whom you mean, is fast asleep by now in her couchette.

WORDSWORTH (3): Then please go double quick tell her Wordsworth here.

HENRY (1): I have no intention of waking her up. If it's money you want, you can take this.

WORDSWORTH (3): I no wan CTC, I wan by bebi gel. You jig-jig with my bebi gel?

HENRY (1): You're preposterous, Wordsworth. She is my aunt. My mother's sister.

WORDSWORTH (3): No humbug?

HENRY (1): No humbug. Even if she were not my aunt, can't you understand that she is a very old lady?

WORDSWORTH (3): No one too old for jig-jig. You tell her she come back here to Paris. Wordsworth wait long long time for her. You tell her she still my bebi gel. Wordsworth no slip good when she gone.

Whistle – Train starts.

SIGN – ORIENT EXPRESS

HENRY (3): I squeezed down the corridor to my aunt's couchette which was number 72. The bed was made up, but there was a strange girl in a mini-skirt sitting on it, while my aunt leant out of the window waving and blowing kisses.

AUNT AUGUSTA (1): Dear man, I had to take a last look. At my age one never knows.

HENRY (3): I thought that chapter was closed, Aunt Augusta.

AUNT AUGUSTA (1): One can never be quite sure. This is 71.

HENRY (1): She indicated the girl who was very young, perhaps eighteen, and who was elaborately made up with a chalk white face.

AUNT AUGUSTA (1): What's your name, dear?

TOOLEY (2): Tooley.

AUNT AUGUSTA (1): Tooley is going to Istanbul too. Aren't you, dear?

TOOLEY (2): En passant.

AUNT AUGUSTA (1): She's going to Katmandu.

HENRY (3): I thought that was in Nepal.

TOOLEY (2): I guess that's where it is. Something like that.

AUNT AUGUSTA (1): She and I got talking because Tooley has brought a sack of provisions with her. Do you realize, Henry, that the Orient Express has no restaurant-car? How times have changed. When I think of the party I once had on this very train with Mr Visconti and General Abdul. Caviar and champagne. We practically lived in the dining car. Now I shall go to bed. You two young people are old enough to be left alone.

SIGN – LYONS

TOOLEY (2): I'm sort of worried, the girl said.

HENRY (1): Anything I can do I replied?

TOOLEY (2): I just want to talk.

HENRY (1): Cigarette?

TOOLEY (2): English?

HENRY (1): Yes.

TOOLEY (2): What does Senior Service mean?

HENRY (1): The Navy.

TOOLEY (2): You don't mind, do you, if I smoke one of my own?

TOOLEY offers joint to HENRY.

HENRY (1): I've never smoked an American cigarette before.

TOOLEY (2): I got these in Paris – from a friend.

HENRY (1): Or French ones.

TOOLEY (2): He was a terribly nice man. Groovy.

HENRY (1): Who was?

TOOLEY (2): This man I met in Paris. I told him my trouble too.

HENRY (1): What is your trouble?

TOOLEY (2): I had a quarrel – with my boyfriend.

HENRY (1): This friend of yours in Paris was a very good judge of cigarettes.

TOOLEY (2): He was fabulous. I mean, he's really together.

HENRY (1): French?

TOOLEY (2): Oh no, he came from darkest Africa.

HENRY (1): A negro?

TOOLEY (2): We don't call them that. We call them coloured or black – whichever they prefer.

HENRY (1): Was he called Wordsworth?

TOOLEY (2): I only knew him as Zach.

HENRY (1): That's the man. Was it you he came to see off at the station?

TOOLEY (2): Sure. Who else? I never expected him, but there he was at the gate to say goodbye.

HENRY (1): He knows my aunt too.

TOOLEY (2): Now isn't that the wildest sort of coincidence? Like something in Thomas Hardy? I'm majoring in English Literature. My father wanted me to take Social Science because he wanted me to serve a while in the Peace Corps.

HENRY (1): What does your father do?

TOOLEY (2): He has a very secret job in the CIA.

HENRY (1): That must be interesting.

TOOLEY (2): He travels about a terrible lot. I haven't seen him more than once since Mum divorced him last fall. What country are we in now?

HENRY (1): I think we must be coming near to the Italian border.

TOOLEY (2): Then open the window quick.

Flaps hankie.

SIGN – ITALY

HENRY (1): What have we been smoking?

TOOLEY (2): Pot, of course. Why?

HENRY (1). Do you realize we could be sent to prison?

TOOLEY (2): I wouldn't be. I'm under age.

HENRY (1): The Italians won't hesitate to imprison someone under age.

TOOLEY (2): Now you're being ironical. I mean I wanted to tell you my great trouble, but how can I do it if you're ironical?

HENRY (1): What's your trouble, Tooley?

TOOLEY (2): I forgot the damn pill and I haven't had the curse for six weeks. Julian said it was my fault – he trusted me.

HENRY (1): Julian is the boyfriend?

TOOLEY (2): Yes, he's a painter and he's fabulous. He was angry because I forgot the pill. He wanted to hitchhike to Istanbul. He said it might do the trick. He gave me an ultimatum. We were in this café and he said, 'We've got to leave now or never', and I said, 'No', and he said, 'Find your own fucking way then'.

HENRY (1): Where is he now?

TOOLEY (2): Somewhere between here and Istanbul.

HENRY (1): How will you find him?

TOOLEY (2): They'll know at the Gulhane.

HENRY (1): What's that?

TOOLEY (2): It's near the Blue Mosque. Everyone knows where everyone is at the Gulhane. I slept with a boy in Paris when Julian walked out because I thought, well, it might stir things up a bit. I mean the curse comes that way sometimes right on top of the orgasm, but I didn't get any orgasm. I guess I was worrying about Julian because I don't often have difficulty that way.

She prepares another joint.

HENRY (1): You oughtn't to smoke that stuff.

TOOLEY (2): Pot? Why? There's no harm in pot. Acid's another thing. Julian wanted me to try acid, but I said not, I mean I don't want to warp my chromosomes.

SIGN – MILAN

HENRY (3): As we left Milan, my aunt said.

AUNT AUGUSTA (1): Mr Visconti found me my situation here in Milan. I grew to be very very fond of him. Fonder than any other man I have ever known. Except the first, but the first is always a special case. But he was a twister, no doubt of it – on one occasion he even ran off with all my money.

HENRY (3): Do you mean he stole it?

AUNT AUGUSTA (1): Yes, I suppose you would put it like that – but Mr Visconti had a scheme for selling fresh vegetables – tomatoes, particularly, of course – to Saudi Arabia. He really believed he would make our fortune. I gave him every penny I possessed. Even his wife lent him a small amount. I shall always remember the conferences at the Ambassador Hotel with Arab notables in long robes who arrived with a dozen wives and a food-taster. It was very romantic while it lasted. Mr Visconti even persuaded the Vatican to put in money, so we had cardinals for cocktails. It was a wonderful sight when the Arabs and the cardinals met, the desert robes and the scarlet skull-caps and all the bowings and embracings and the kissing of rings. Everybody enjoyed these parties, but only the Arabs, as it turned out, could really afford their fun.

HENRY (3): Was Mr Visconti ruined?

AUNT AUGUSTA (1): He pulled out in time with what was left of my money. He disappeared and I went to live in Rome. Life was very middle-class after all the Arabs and the cardinals. And then – Oh praise to the Holiest in the height, as Wordsworth is fond of saying – I was putting in a little part-time work in the establishment behind the Messaggero when who should walk in but Mr Visconti. A pure coincidence. He wasn't looking for me. But how happy we were. The girls didn't understand when we joined hands then and there and danced between the sofas.

HENRY (3): What was that part-time employment? Who were the girls? What were the sofas there for?

AUNT AUGUSTA (1): What does it matter now? What did any of it matter? We were together again.

HENRY (3): But surely you must have despised the man after all he had done to you?

AUNT AUGUSTA (1): I despise no one, no one. Never presume yours is a better morality. What do you suppose I was doing in the house behind the Messaggero? I was cheating, wasn't I? So why shouldn't Mr Visconti cheat me? But you, I suppose, never cheated in all your little provincial banker's life because there's not anything you wanted enough, not even money, not even a woman. My sister certainly brought you up as she wanted you. Your poor father didn't have a chance. He was a cheat too, and I only wish you were.

HENRY (3): I think I'd better find Tooley. Later as we left Venice, Tooley said.

SIGN – VENICE

TOOLEY (2): Mr Pulling, would you mind getting me some more coke?

HENRY (1): There's nowhere on the train to keep it cold.

TOOLEY (2): I don't mind warm coke. Julian did a fabulous picture of a coke bottle once. He painted it bright yellow. Fauve. He wants to do a series of enormous pictures of Heinz soups in fabulous colours.

HENRY (1): Surely somebody once did paint a Heinz soup tin?

TOOLEY (2): Not Heinz, Campbell's. That was Andy Warhol. I said the same thing. But Julian said that wasn't the point. He said that there are certain subjects which belong to a certain period and culture. Like the Annunciation did. Botticelli wasn't put off because Piero della Francesca had done the same thing.

SIGN – YUGOSLAVIA

HENRY (3): I'm sorry about yesterday afternoon, Aunt Augusta, I said. I really didn't mean to say anything against Mr Visconti. After all I don't know the circumstances.

AUNT AUGUSTA (1): He was a quite impossible man, but I loved him and what he did with my money was the least of his faults. For example he was what they call a collaborator. During the German occupation he acted as adviser to the German authorities on questions of art and the acquisition of paintings, and he had to get out of Italy very quickly after the death of Mussolini.

SIGN – FLASHBACK ROME 1944

Noises – bombardment, jeeps, tanks, distant guns, marching feet, shouted orders in German.

AUNT AUGUSTA (1): He certainly escaped the hard way. When the Allies were coming close, Mr Visconti went to a clerical store in Rome and paid a fortune to be fitted out like a

priest, a monsignor in fact. Then he went with a suitcase
to the lavatory in the Excelsior Hotel to change. Well, in
those days a lot of girls used to come to the bar of the hotel
to pick up German officers. One of the girls – I suppose
it was the approach of the Allied troops that did it – was
having a crise de conscience. She regretted her lost purity,
she would never sin again. Then she spied Mr Visconti.

ITALIAN GIRL (2): Monsignor, hear my confession.

VISCONTI (3): My child, this is no fit place for a confession.

ITALIAN GIRL (2). What does the place matter? We are all
about to die, and I am in mortal sin. Please, Monsignor.

VISCONTI (3): My child, in this state of emergency a simple act
of contrition is enough.

ITALIAN GIRL (2): Father, help me.

VISCONTI (3): How many times, my child?

ITALIAN GIRL (2): How can you ask that, Father? I've been at
it all the time ever since the occupation. After all they were
our allies, Father.

VISCONTI (3): Always the same thing, my child?

ITALIAN GIRL (2): Of course not, Father. Who on earth do you
think I am?

VISCONTI (3): Anything unnatural, my child?

ITALIAN GIRL (2): What do you mean unnatural, Father?

Visconti whispers something to her.

Surely that's not unnatural, Father?

AUNT AUGUSTA (1): A German officer came in and told the
monsignor to hurry up. He had a more important customer
for him. It was the wife of the German General who
had come down to the bar for a last dry Martini before

escaping north. She drained her Martini in one gulp and commanded the confession.

FRAU GENERAL (2): Adultery. Three times.

VISCONTI (3): Are you married, my daughter?

FRAU GENERAL (2): Of course I'm married. What on earth do you suppose? I'm Frau General Schmidt.

VISCONTI (3): Does your husband know of this?

FRAU GENERAL (2): Of course he doesn't know. He's not a priest.

VISCONTI (3): Then you have been guilty of lies too?

FRAU GENERAL (2): Yes, yes, naturally, I suppose so, you must hurry, Father. Our car's being loaded. We are leaving for Florence in a few minutes.

VISCONTI (3): Have you missed Mass?

FRAU GENERAL (2): Oh, occasionally, Father. This is war-time. Those are allied planes overhead. We have to leave immediately.

VISCONTI (3): God cannot be hurried, my child. Have you indulged in impure thoughts?

FRAU GENERAL (2): Father, put down yes to anything you like, but give me absolution. I have to be off.

VISCONTI (3): I cannot feel that you've properly examined your conscience.

FRAU GENERAL (2): Unless you give me absolution at once, I shall have you shot. For sabotage.

VISCONTI (3): It would be better if you gave me a seat in your car. We could finish your confession tonight.

FRAU GENERAL (2): There isn't room in the car, Father. The driver, my husband, myself, my dog –

VISCONTI (3): A dog takes up no room. It can sit on your knee.

FRAU GENERAL (2): This is an Irish wolfhound, Father.

VISCONTI (3): Then you must leave it behind.

FRAU GENERAL (2): I need Wolf for my protection, Father. War is very dangerous for women.

VISCONTI (3): Then I suggest that we leave your husband behind.

AUNT AUGUSTA (1): And so it came about. The Frau General seated herself beside the driver and Mr Visconti sat beside Wolf at the back.

FRAU GENERAL (2): Drive off.

AUNT AUGUSTA (1): The driver hesitated, but he was more afraid of the wife than the husband. The General came out into the street and shouted to them as they drove off – a tank had stopped to give precedence to the staff car. Nobody paid any attention to the General's shouts except Wolf.

Actor (4) becomes Wolf and acts out what AUNT AUGUSTA is describing.

He clambered all over Mr Visconti, thrusting his evil-smelling parts against Mr Visconti's face, barking furiously to get out. Blindly Mr Visconti fumbled for the handle of the window. Before it was properly open Wolf jumped right in the path of the following tank. It flattened him. Mr Visconti looking back thought that he resembled one of those biscuits they make for children in the shape of animals.

SIGN – BACK ON TRAIN

HENRY (2): What happened to Mr Visconti in the end?

AUNT AUGUSTA (1): I thought for a long time he'd been liquidated by the partisans, but Mr Visconti was great at survival. Why, the old sod, he survives to this moment. That's why you and I have taken the train to see General Abdul.

HENRY (2): But where is Mr Visconti?

AUNT AUGUSTA (1): It's better you shouldn't know, there are people still after him.

SIGN – TURKEY

HENRY (3): I'm awfully afraid that Tooley's going to have a baby.

AUNT AUGUSTA (1): She ought to take precautions, Henry, but in any case it's far too early for you to worry.

HENRY (3): Good heavens, Aunt Augusta, I didn't mean that… how can you possibly think…?

AUNT AUGUSTA (1): It's a natural conclusion, you have been much together. And the girl has a certain puppy charm.

HENRY (3): I'm too old for that sort of thing.

AUNT AUGUSTA (1): You are a young man in your fifties.

HENRY (3): The door clanged, and there was Tooley, but a Tooley transformed.

TOOLEY (2): Good morning, good morning. Oh, Mr Pulling, it's happened.

HENRY (1): What's happened?

TOOLEY (2): The curse. I've got the curse. I was right, you see. The jolting of the train, I mean – it did do it. I've got a terrible belly-ache, but I feel fabulous. I can't wait to tell Julian. Oh, I hope he's at the Gulhane, when I get there. You've been so kind, Mr Pulling. I don't know what I'd have done without you. I mean it was a bit like the dark night of the soul. I'll be seeing you both again before we go, won't I?

HENRY (1): But she didn't. She had become one of the young now, and I could only wave to her back as she went ahead of us through the customs. My responsibility was over, but she stayed on in my memory like a small persistent pain which worries even in its insignificance.

SIGN – PERA PALACE HOTEL, ISTANBUL

HENRY (2): There was no message waiting for my aunt at the hotel, and no one called all evening. Can't you telephone General Abdul, I asked?

AUNT AUGUSTA (1): Even in the early days, he never trusted his own line.

Telephone rings.

Perhaps it's General Abdul at last. Though eleven at night seems late.

RECEPTIONIST (4): This is reception.

AUNT AUGUSTA (1): Yes, what is it?

RECEPTIONIST (4): I am sorry to disturb you, Miss Bertram, but Colonel Hakim of the Turkish Police wishes to see you. He is on the way up now.

AUNT AUGUSTA (1): A police officer? I begin to think I am back in the old days. With Mr Visconti. Henry, will you open my suitcase? You'll find a light coat there.

HENRY (2): Yes, Aunt Augusta.

AUNT AUGUSTA (1): Under the coat in a cardboard box you will find a candle – a decorated candle. Take out the candle, but be careful because it's rather heavy. Put it on my bedside table and light it. Candlelight is better for my complexion.

HAKIM (3): Miss Bertram?

AUNT AUGUSTA (1): Yes. You are Colonel Hakim?

HAKIM (3): Yes. I am sorry to call on you so late without warning. I think we have a mutual acquaintance, General Abdul. May I turn on the light, Miss Bertram?

AUNT AUGUSTA (1): I would rather not. I have weak eyes, and I always prefer to read by candlelight.

HAKIM (3): A very beautiful candle.

AUNT AUGUSTA (1): They make them in Venice. The coats of arms belong to their four greatest doges. How is General Abdul? I had been hoping to meet him again.

HAKIM (3): I am afraid General Abdul is a very sick man.

AUNT AUGUSTA (1): What is wrong with him?

HAKIM (3): He was shot while trying to escape.

AUNT AUGUSTA (1): Escape? Escape from whom?

HAKIM (3): From me. He was a great friend of you and Mr Visconti, was he not? Where is Mr Visconti now?

AUNT AUGUSTA (1): I've no idea.

HAKIM (3): Nor had General Abdul. We only want the information for the Interpol files. It is not the real subject of my interrogation.

AUNT AUGUSTA (1): Am I being interrogated, Colonel?

HAKIM (3): Yes. In a way. I hope an agreeable way. We have found a letter from you to General Abdul which speaks about an investment he had recommended. General Abdul was planning a little trouble here, a little 'take over' or coup; he was very short of funds. So he got in touch with you, perhaps he hoped through you to contact Visconti again? He was offering the attractive but unlikely interest rate of twenty-five per cent.

AUNT AUGUSTA (1): Mr Visconti would certainly have seen through that.

HAKIM (3): But now you are a lady living alone. You might be tempted a little by the quick profits... Or perhaps by the sense of adventure.

AUNT AUGUSTA (1): At my age?

HAKIM (3): Would you mind if we search the room? Would you mind if I put on the electric light?

AUNT AUGUSTA (1). I would mind a great deal, I left my dark glasses on the train. Unless you wish to give me a splitting headache...

HAKIM (3): Of course not, Miss Bertram. We will do without.

HENRY (2): They searched the room with great thoroughness, under the bed, behind the drawers, in all the suitcases – everywhere.

HAKIM (3): Well, we have found nothing compromising in your luggage. And now Mr Pulling's pockets.

HAKIM and policeman frisk HENRY savagely.

I will say goodnight now, Miss Bertram. You have made my duty tonight a most agreeable one. I will send a police car to take you to your plane tomorrow.

AUNT AUGUSTA (1): Please don't bother. We can take a taxi.

HAKIM (3): We should be sorry to see you miss your plane.

HENRY (2): Aunt Augusta, what did all that mean?

AUNT AUGUSTA (1): Some little political trouble, I would imagine. Politics in Turkey are taken more seriously than they are at home. It was only quite recently that they executed a Prime Minister. We dream of it, but they act. I hadn't realized, I admit, what General Abdul was up to. Foolish of him at his age to attempt a coup.

HENRY (2): Do you realize that they're deporting us?

AUNT AUGUSTA (1): You exaggerate, dear. They are just lending us a police car.

HENRY (2): And if we refuse to take it?

AUNT AUGUSTA (1): I have no intention of refusing. We were already booked on the plane. After making my investment here I had no intention of lingering around. I didn't expect quick profits, and twenty-five per cent always involves a risk.

HENRY (2): What investment, Aunt Augusta? Forty pounds in travellers' cheques?

AUNT AUGUSTA (1): Oh no, dear. I bought quite a large gold ingot in Paris. You remember the man from the bank…

HENRY (2): So that was what they were looking for. Where on earth had you hidden it? My eye fell on the large ornamented candle.

AUNT AUGUSTA (1): Yes, dear, how clever of you to guess. Colonel Hakim didn't. You can blow it out now.

HENRY (2): What do you propose to do with this now?

AUNT AUGUSTA (1): I shall have to take it back to England with me. It may be of use another time.

HENRY (2): Why on earth did you do it? Such a risk…

AUNT AUGUSTA (1): Mr Visconti is in need of money.

HENRY (2): He stole yours.

AUNT AUGUSTA (1): That was a long time ago. He will have spent it all by now.

SIGN – SOUTHWOOD

HENRY (2): It seemed at first another and a happier world which I had re-entered: I was back home.

HENRY (1): A package of Omo was propped against the scraper. I had certainly not ordered any detergent. I looked closer and saw that it was a gift package.

HENRY (3): I went into the garden. My next door neighbour had neglected the dahlias.

HENRY (2): The afternoon post arrived punctually at five: it included a letter with a South African stamp.

HENRY (3). I saw at once that it came from Miss Keene. She had bought herself a typewriter, but it was obvious that as yet she had not had much practice.

MISS KEENE (2): We drove to Koffiefontein – three hours by road – to a matinee of Gone with the Qind. Clark Fable was not as good as I remembered him. I miss very much St John's Church and the vicar's sermons. The only church near here is Dutch Deformed, and I don't like it at all. I look forward so to your letters…

HENRY (1): I wondered how I was to reply. I knew that the letter she would like best would contain the small details of every day, even to the condition of my dahlias. How was I to deal with my bizarre journey to Istanbul?

HENRY (3): I went to choose a book from my shelves. I opened Rob Roy and found a snapshot lying between the leaves: the square yellowing snapshot of a pretty girl in an old-fashioned bathing-dress taken with an old-fashioned Brownie. The girl was bending a little towards the camera; she had just slipped one shoulder out of its strap, and she was laughing, as though she had been surprised at the moment of changing.

HENRY (1): It was some moments before I recognized Aunt Augusta and my first thought was how attractive she had been in those days. Was it a photograph taken by her sister, I wondered? But it was hardly the kind of photograph my mother would have given my father. I had to admit that it was more likely he had taken it himself and hidden it there in a volume of Scott. She had an air of being ready for anything.

HENRY (2): I thought of my father with an added tenderness – of that lazy man lying in his overcoat in the empty bath.

Telephone.

Aunt Augusta, I have been thinking. I don't know why, of my father. It's strange how little one knows of one's own family. Do you realize I don't even know where he is buried. Do you?

AUNT AUGUSTA (1): Of course.

HENRY (2): I would have liked, if only once, to visit his grave.

AUNT AUGUSTA (1): Cemeteries to me are rather a morbid taste. They have a sour smell like jungles.

HENRY (2): Where is my father?

AUNT AUGUSTA (1): As a half-believing Catholic, I cannot answer that question with any certainty, but his body, what is left of it, lies in Boulogne.

HENRY (2): Perhaps one day we might go together.

AUNT AUGUSTA (1): I am always ready to visit a new place and I have often wondered what on earth your father was doing in Boulogne out of season?

SIGN – THE CEMETERY, BOULOGNE

Rain, umbrellas, wreath.

HENRY (1): We were directed to my father's grave. As we approached, we saw a small elderly woman in black standing beside it. How odd! There seems to be another mourner.

HENRY (2): The little woman looked at us with astonishment.

MISS PATERSON (3): Qui etes-vous?

AUNT AUGUSTA (1): Who are you?

HENRY (1): My aunt demanded bluntly.

MISS PATERSON (3): Miss Paterson.

AUNT AUGUSTA (1): And what has this grave to do with you?

MISS PATERSON (3): I have come here once a month for more than forty years.

AUNT AUGUSTA (1): Did you know my brother-in-law?

MISS PATERSON (3): Your brother-in-law!

AUNT AUGUSTA (1): And this, my good woman, is Richard Pulling's son.

MISS PATERSON (3): The family.

HENRY (2): I think it is very kind of you to lay flowers on my father's grave. It may seem strange to you that I have never been here before...

MISS PATERSON (3): It is quite typical of you all, of you all. Your mother never even came to the funeral. I was the only one. I and the concierge of the hotel. A kind man. It was a wet, wet day, and he brought his big umbrella...

HENRY (2): Then you knew my father... You were here...?

AUNT AUGUSTA (1): When did you meet my brother-in-law?

MISS PATERSON (3): We met on the top of a 49 bus.

AUNT AUGUSTA (1): A 49 bus?

MISS PATERSON (3): Yes, you see, I had heard him ask for his ticket and when his destination came he was fast asleep, so I woke him up. He was very grateful and came all the way to Chelsea Town Hall with me. I had a basement room in Oakley Street and he walked back to the house with me. I remember it all so clearly, so clearly, as though it were only yesterday. We found many things in common.

AUNT AUGUSTA (1): That surprises me.

MISS PATERSON (3): Oh how we talked that day!

HENRY (2): What about?

MISS PATERSON (3): Mainly I think about Sir Walter Scott. I knew *Marmion* and little else, but he knew everything that Sir Walter had ever written. He had a wonderful memory for poetry. 'Where shall the traitor rest, He the deceiver, Who could win maiden's breast, Ruin and leave her?'

AUNT AUGUSTA (1): And the traitor rests in Boulogne.

MISS PATERSON (3): He wanted to give me a holiday. He said I needed sea air. Just a day trip. We took the boat to Calais, for he wanted to show me where the six burghers came from, and then we took a bus here to see the Napoleon column – and we found there was no boat back from Boulogne.

AUNT AUGUSTA (1): That came as a surprise to him, I suppose?

MISS PATERSON (3): Yes. He was very apologetic. However we found two clean rooms in a little inn up in the high town in the square.

AUNT AUGUSTA (1): Adjoining rooms, I assume.

MISS PATERSON (3): Yes, because I was frightened.

HENRY (2): Of what?

MISS PATERSON (3): I had never been abroad before, nor had Mr Pulling. In the middle of the night I heard him knock on the door and call – Dolly?

AUNT AUGUSTA (1): Dolly!

MISS PATERSON (3): Yes. That was what he called me. My name is Dorothy.

AUNT AUGUSTA (1): You had locked your door, of course.

MISS PATERSON (3): I had done no such thing. He was a man I trusted absolutely. I told him to come in. I knew he wouldn't have woken me for any trivial reason.

AUNT AUGUSTA (1): Certainly I would not describe his reason as trivial. Go on.

MISS PATERSON (3): He came in and he whispered – Dolly, my darling – and he fell down on the floor. I got down beside him and put his poor poor head in my lap and he never spoke again. I never knew why he came or what he meant to say to me.

AUNT AUGUSTA (1): I can guess.

MISS PATERSON (3): I hope you are right. I know well what you are thinking and I hope you are right. I would have done anything that he asked me without hesitation or regret. And I have never loved another man.

AUNT AUGUSTA (1): You didn't have the time to love him, it seems.

MISS PATERSON (3): There you are quite wrong. Perhaps because you don't know what love is. I loved him from the moment he got off the bus at Chelsea Town Hall, and I love him today.

AUNT AUGUSTA (1): You have certainly been very constant.

MISS PATERSON (3): No one else has ever again used that name he called me, Dolly. But in the war when I had to use an alias, I let them call me Poupee.

HENRY (2): Why on earth did you need an alias?

MISS PATERSON (3): I have always lived here since Richard died. Mr Pulling, I mean.

HENRY (2): Even during the war?

MISS PATERSON (3): It was a time of some privation, but the people here were very good to me. I was protected. The mayor provided me with an identity card. After the war they even gave me a medal.

AUNT AUGUSTA (1): What for?

MISS PATERSON (3): Various things. They were troubled times.

Miss Paterson leaves.

AUNT AUGUSTA (1): You were quite taken by that miserable little woman.

HENRY (2): I was touched to meet someone who loved my father.

AUNT AUGUSTA (1): A lot of women loved him.

HENRY (2): I mean a woman who really loved him.

AUNT AUGUSTA (1): The woman seemed to me totally inadequate to her grief. She irritated me. To think that she was with your father when he died. Little sentimental creature, she doesn't know what love is.

HENRY (2): Do you?

AUNT AUGUSTA (1): I think I have had rather more experience of it than you.

HENRY (2): My aunt did not return with me to England.

HENRY (3): I saw her off at the station and received the coldest of cold pecks upon the cheek.

HENRY (1): She gave me the keys to her apartment.

AUNT AUGUSTA (1): If I am away a long time, I may want you to send me something or just to look in to see that all is well.

SIGN – SOUTHWOOD

HENRY (2): A month passed and no news came to me from my aunt. I rang several times, but there was never any reply.

I tried to interest myself in a novel of Thackeray's, but it lacked the immediacy of my aunt's stories.

HENRY picks up pile of mail.

HENRY (3): When six weeks went by without news I became anxious. I had lost the taste for dahlias. When weeds swarmed up I was tempted to let them grow.

HENRY (1): Christmas approached with no news of my aunt. (*Finds Tooley's card.*) But there was a postcard from Tooley. It was the view of a rather ugly temple in Katmandu.

TOOLEY (2): I am on a marvellous trip. Love and peace, Tooley.

HENRY (2): I decided to visit my aunt's apartment at the Crown and Anchor.

SIGN – THE FLAT

When I opened the door of the flat I found everything in deep darkness. I set a table rocking and something Venetian tinkled into fragments on the floor. When I drew the curtains the Venetian glasses had no glitter – they had gone dead like unused pearls.

HENRY (3): In Wordsworth's room the bed had been stripped. The only decoration left was a framed photograph of Freetown harbour which showed market women in bright dresses with baskets on their heads. I hadn't noticed it when I came before.

HENRY (1): I returned to the sitting room and began to go through the post.

SPARROW (3): Forgive us coming in without ringing, Mr Pulling.

HENRY (1): Detective-Sergeant Sparrow?

SPARROW (3): It is just as well we have found you here.

POLICEMAN (2): The door being open…

SPARROW (3): I have a search warrant. All the same we prefer a member of the family to be present at a search.

HENRY (1): What have you got against my aunt?

SPARROW (3): Have you ever heard of a Mr Visconti?

HENRY (1): The name is somehow familiar.

SPARROW (3): A war criminal and General Abdul – you've heard of General Abdul, I presume?

HENRY (1): … Perhaps, yes, I seem to know the name.

SPARROW (3): General Abdul made a statement before he died.

HENRY (1): Died? Poor fellow. I didn't know. I can't see how his statement can concern me.

SPARROW (3): The statement concerned Mr Visconti. Interpol has circulated the details. Until now we had always assumed that Mr Visconti was dead. We had written him off.

POLICEMAN (2): This man Visconti, sir. He's a viper.

HENRY (1): They trailed from room to room and I followed them. I thought they were less thorough in their search than Colonel Hakim.

POLICEMAN (2): All this glass, curious stuff. It's like a museum.

SPARROW (3): Collectors' pieces? Works of art?

HENRY (1): It's a matter of taste.

SPARROW (3): Any pictures?

HENRY (1): Only a photo of Freetown harbour.

SPARROW (3): Why Freetown?

HENRY (1): Wordsworth came from there.

SPARROW (3): It's a good-looking frame. Cost more than the photograph.

POLICEMAN (2): Italian too from the look of it, like the glass. Perhaps given her by the man Visconti?

SPARROW (3): There's no indication on the back. I had hoped for an inscription.

POLICEMAN (2): Have you ever heard your aunt mention any of these names – Tiberio Titi?

HENRY (1): No.

POLICEMAN (2): Stradano? Passerati? Cossa? Leonard O. da Vinci?

HENRY (1): No. She's never spoken to me very much about her Italian friends.

SPARROW (3): These weren't friends. If you hear from your aunt, if you ever do, please ring us at once.

HENRY (1): I promise nothing.

POLICEMAN (2): It is possible that she might be in serious personal danger. From her unfortunate associations.

SPARROW (3): Particularly from that viper Visconti.

HENRY (1): Why do you keep calling him a viper?

SPARROW (3): It's the only description Interpol has given us. He was once described as a viper by the Chief of Police in Rome in 1945, and we don't know now whether viper was a physical description or what you might call a moral judgement.

HENRY (1): When I double-locked the door and left the Crown and Anchor, I had the sad impression that my aunt might be dead and the most interesting part of my life might be over. During that empty time I received another letter from Miss Keene.

MISS KEENE (2): Sometimes I fear that I am going to be quite assimilated. In Koffiefontein the Prime Minister no longer seems the monster we thought him at home: indeed he's criticized here sometimes as an old-fashioned liberal. I have met a Mr Hughes, a land surveyor, and he wants to marry me – please don't laugh at me. He is a kind man in his late fifties, a widower. I don't know what to do. It would be the final assimilation, wouldn't it? I've always had a silly dream of one day coming back to Southwood and beginning my life all over again. I wish you were not so far away, for I know you would counsel me wisely.

HENRY (3): Was I wrong to read an appeal in the last sentence, an appeal for some decisive telegram 'Come back to Southwood and marry me'? Who knows whether I might not have sent one in my loneliness if another letter had not arrived?

HENRY (2): (*Reading letter.*) Hotel Lancaster, Buenos Aires?

AUNT AUGUSTA (1): I have decided not to return to Europe and I am giving up my apartment over the Crown and Anchor. I would be glad if you would dispose of all the furniture. On second thoughts however keep the photograph of Freetown harbour and bring it with you. Preserve it in its frame which has great sentimental value because it was given me by Mr V. I enclose a first-class ticket to Buenos Aires. Come as soon as you can, for I get no younger.

HENRY (3): I telegraphed to Miss Keene –

HENRY (2): Joining my aunt in Buenos Aires shortly. Will write.

SIGN – INTERVAL

Act Two

SIGN – ARGENTINA

Music – South American.

HENRY (3): There was no one to meet me at the airport, and when I arrived at the hotel, I found only a letter.

AUNT AUGUSTA (1): I am sorry not to be here to greet you in Argentina but I have had to move on urgently to Paraguay where an old friend of mine is in some distress. I have left you a ticket for the river-boat. I will see that you are met.

HENRY (3): It was a highly unsatisfactory arrangement.

HENRY (2): There were© four days ahead of me, up the Plata, the Parana and the Paraguay. I left the Argentine winter for my over-heated cabin.

Ship's hooter.

HENRY (3): I propped the photograph of Freetown harbour at the back of my dressing-table and supported it with my books.

HENRY (2): I had brought with me Palgrave's Golden Treasury, the collected poems of Tennyson and Wordsworth, and I had added Rob Roy, perhaps because it contained the only photograph I possessed of my aunt.

HENRY (1): I found myself thinking not for the first time that the happy smile, the young breasts, the curve of her body in the old-fashioned bathing-costume were like the suggestion of a budding maternity.

HENRY (3): I finished my unpacking and went down to the bar.

HENRY (1): A rabbit-nosed man with a long drooping moustache approached me.

SPANISH GENTLEMAN (3): Perdone, estimado Sênor, pero le puedo molestar?

HENRY (1): No hablo Español, Sênor.

SPANISH GENTLEMAN (3): Me gustaria mucho leer en las lineas de su mano. Para mi seria un gran placer.

O'TOOLE (2): Can I be of any help?

HENRY (2): Said a tall, sad, grey American whom I hadn't noticed as we came on board.

HENRY (1): I don't understand what this gentleman wants.

O'TOOLE (2): His hobby is reading hands.

HENRY (1): I don't mind.

SPANISH GENTLEMAN (3): Usted he venido de muy lejos.

O'TOOLE (2): He says you have come from a long way off.

HENRY (1): That's a bit obvious, isn't it?

SPANISH GENTLEMAN (3): Sus viajes llegaran pronto a su fin.

O'TOOLE (2): But your travels are nearly over.

HENRY (1): That can hardly be true. I have to go back home.

SPANISH GENTLEMAN (3): Preveo que encontrera de nuevo con una persona que siempre le ha estado muy cerco. Puede que sea su mujer.

O'TOOLE (2): He sees a reunion of someone very close to you. Your wife perhaps.

HENRY (1): I have no wife.

SPANISH GENTLEMAN (3): O puede que sea su madre.

O'TOOLE (2): He says it could be your mother.

HENRY (1): She's dead. At least…

SPANISH GENTLEMAN (3): Preveo a la muerte, pero esta muy lejos de la linea de su corazon.

O'TOOLE (2): He sees a death – but it's far away from your heart-line. It's not an important death.

HENRY (1): Do you believe in this nonsense?

O'TOOLE (2): No, I guess not, but I try to keep an open mind. My name's O'Toole, James O'Toole.

HENRY (1): Mine's Pulling – Henry.

O'TOOLE (2): You a Londoner, Henry?

HENRY (1): Yes.

O'TOOLE (2): I come from Philadelphia. Mind if I join you?

Actor (4) serves drink to O'Toole.

You going to Asuncion too?

HENRY (1): Yes.

O'TOOLE (2): There's nowhere else on this trip worth a visit. Formosa – that's a dump. Only smugglers get off there. I guess you're not a smuggler?

HENRY (1): No. You seem to know these parts well.

O'TOOLE (2): Too well. You on vacation, Henry?

HENRY (1): I suppose so. Yes.

O'TOOLE (2): All by yourself? Not much fun. Strange country. And you don't speak the language – not that Spanish is any good outside the city. In the country they all speak Guarani.

HENRY (1): Do you?

O'TOOLE (2): A smattering, Henry.

HENRY (1): I am visiting an old relation of mine, James.

O'TOOLE (2): My friends call me Tooley.

HENRY (1): Are you in business here?

O'TOOLE (2): Not exactly, I do research work. Social research. You know the sort of thing, Henry. Cost of living. Malnutrition. Degree of illiteracy. Have a drink.

HENRY (1): Do you find things easy in Paraguay? I've read in the papers you Americans have a lot of trouble in South America.

O'TOOLE (2): Not in Paraguay. We and the General are like that.

HENRY (1): He's quite a tough dictator, so they tell me.

O'TOOLE (2): It's what the country needs, Henry. A strong hand. Don't mistake me though. I keep out of politics. Simple research. That's my line. I've got to take a leak.

They pee together.

HENRY (1): Are you married, Tooley?

O'TOOLE (2): Yeah. Sort of.

HENRY (1): You've got a daughter?

O'TOOLE (2): Sure. Why? She's studying in London.

HENRY (1): She's in Katmandu.

O'TOOLE (2): Katmandu! Why, that's Nepal. That's a hell of a thing to tell me. How do you know?

HENRY (3): I told him about the Orient Express.

O'TOOLE (2): What can I do, Henry? I've got my work. I can't go chasing round the world. Lucinda doesn't know the worry she gives.

HENRY (1): Lucinda? She calls herself Tooley now like you.

O'TOOLE (2): She does? That's new.

HENRY (1): She has a great admiration for you. She told me you were in the CIA.

O'TOOLE (2): She's a romantic. She imagines things.

HENRY (1): Is the CIA romantic?

O'TOOLE (2): A kid thinks so. I guess she saw some file of mine marked Secret. Everything's secret here. Even a report on malnutrition in Asuncion.

HENRY (1): Is that what you are researching?

O'TOOLE (2): I've never told anyone about this, Henry. The fact is I count while I'm pissing and then I write down how long I've taken and what time it is. Do you realize we spend more than one whole day a year pissing?

HENRY (1): Good heavens.

O'TOOLE (2): I can prove it, Henry. Look here. July 28, 7.15, .17 seconds, 10.45, .37 seconds, 12.30, .50 seconds – and so on – total for the day, four minutes thirty-one seconds. That makes half an hour a week. Twenty-six hours a year.

HENRY (1): Are you drawing any conclusions?

O'TOOLE (2): That's not my job. I just report the facts. It's for others to draw the conclusions.

HENRY (1): Who are the others?

O'TOOLE (2): Well, I thought when I had completed six months' research I'd get in touch with a urinary specialist. Those guys deal all the time with the sick. It's important to them to know what happens in the case of an average fellow.

HENRY (1): And you are the average fellow?

O'TOOLE (2): Yes. I'm one hundred per cent healthy, Henry. I have to be in my job. They give me the works every so often.

HENRY (1): The CIA.

O'TOOLE (2): You're kidding, Henry. You can't believe that crazy girl.

SIGN – FORMOSA, ARGENTINA

HENRY (2): It was two days later. We turned off the great Parana river.

HENRY (3): Fifty yards across the water from Formosa lay Paraguay sodden and empty.

HENRY (1): It certainly seemed an ideal town for smugglers with only a river to cross.

HENRY (2): I was tired of walking the deck, so I went ashore too.

HENRY (3): The pervading smell of orange petals was the only sweet thing about Formosa.

HENRY (1): The only old and beautiful building in the long avenue proved, as I came closer to it, to be the prison.

SIGN – REVERIE

All three on a park bench.

HENRY (2): I sat on a bench outside it and remembered my father's favourite poem 'The Ode on Immortality'.

HENRY (3): When I first entered the bank as a junior clerk I had thought of it in Wordsworth's terms as a 'prison-house'.

HENRY (2): I can remember very little of the vision preceding the prison-house; it must have faded very early into the 'light of common day', but it seemed to me that my aunt for one had never allowed the vision to fade. Perhaps a sense of morality is the sad compensation we learn to enjoy, like a remission for good conduct. In the vision there is no morality.

HENRY (1): I was born as a result of what my stepmother would have called an immoral act, an act of darkness. I had begun in immoral freedom. Why then should I have found myself in a prison-house? How ambiguous my feelings were. I thought of Miss Keene and her letter of shy appeal, of my home in Southwood, of my garden, of the sweet sound of the bells from Church Road. A little world of aging people where one read of danger only in the newspaper. I rose to return to the boat.

WORDSWORTH (3): Mr Pullen. Mr Pullen.

HENRY (1): Why, Wordsworth, what on earth are you doing here?

WORDSWORTH (3): My lil bebi gel, she tell me go Formosa and wait for Mr Pullen come.

HENRY (1): How is my aunt, Wordsworth?

WORDSWORTH (3): She pretty ok. She dance one hell too much. Ar tell her she no bebi gel no more... Man, she got me real worried.

HENRY (1): Are you coming on the boat with me?

WORDSWORTH (3): Ar sure am, Mr Pullen. You lef everyting to old Wordsworth. Ar know the customs fellows in Asuncion. Some good guys. Some bad like hell. You lef me talk.

HENRY (1): I'm not smuggling anything, Wordsworth.

WORDSWORTH (3): You got that picture, Mr Pullen?

HENRY (1): You mean of Freetown harbour? Yes, I've got that.

WORDSWORTH (3): Ar lak you, Mr Pullen. You allays straight with old Wordsworth. You got CTC for Wordsworth?

Ship's hooter.

O'TOOLE (2): What did you think of Formosa?

HENRY (1): There wasn't much to see.

O'TOOLE (2): Met a friend, didn't you?

HENRY (1): A friend?

O'TOOLE (2): I saw you talking to a coloured guy.

HENRY (1): Oh, he wanted money. I didn't see you on shore.

O'TOOLE (2): I was up on the bridge looking through the captain's glasses.

HENRY (1): How are the urine statistics?

O'TOOLE (2): More than four minutes thirty seconds today. So you didn't like Formosa?

HENRY (1): No. Of course it may be all right for fishing.

O'TOOLE (2): Fishing! Smuggling is what you mean.

HENRY (1): I keep on hearing all the time about smuggling.

O'TOOLE (2): It's the national industry of Paraguay. It brings in nearly as much as the maté and a lot more than hiding war criminals.

HENRY (1): What have they got to smuggle?

O'TOOLE (2): Scotch whisky and American cigarettes. You get yourself an agent in Panama who buys wholesale and he flies the stuff down to Paraguay, then you transfer the crates to a private plane. You'd be surprised to see how many private Dakotas there are now in Asuncion. Then your pilot takes off to Argentina just across the river. A few hundred kilometres from Buenos Aires you touch down, unload into trucks and there you are. You tempted, Henry?

HENRY (1): I didn't have the right training at the bank.

O'TOOLE (2): The risks are big too for a foreigner. There's hijacking. Or the police get greedy. Who's going to make a fuss about an odd body or two? They don't have coroners in Paraguay.

HENRY (1): And I suppose the CIA aren't interested?

O'TOOLE (2): You shouldn't believe that nonsense, Henry. I told you – Lucinda's a romantic.

HENRY (1): I returned to my cabin. I hadn't locked my door, and yet it wouldn't open when I pushed.

WORDSWORTH (3): Come in, boss.

HENRY (1): How can I come in?

HENRY (3): He had wedged the door with a chair. He removed it now and let me in.

WORDSWORTH (3): Ar got to be careful, Mr Pullen.

HENRY (1): Careful of what?

WORDSWORTH (3): Too much bad people on this boat, too much humbug.

HENRY (1): Yes, yes, that's fine, but what are you doing barricaded in my cabin?

WORDSWORTH (3): Ar come for the picture.

HENRY (1): Couldn't you wait till we get ashore?

WORDSWORTH (3): Your auntie say bring that picture safe, Wordsworth, double quick or you no come here no more.

HENRY (1): A suspicion returned to me. Could the frame like the candle be made of gold? Or did the photograph cover some notes of a very high denomination? It's only a photograph of Freetown harbour.

WORDSWORTH (3): Ya'as, Mr Pullen. But your auntie say...

HENRY (1): All right. Take it then.

WORDSWORTH (3): Ar got a lot o' worry about your auntie, Mr Pullen. She was allays safe with old Wordsworth. Ar no cost her nothing. But she got a fellah now – he cost her plenty plenty. What for she leave Wordsworth for a man like him? Tell me that, man, tell me that. She war my bebi gel. Now she gon bust ma heart in bits.

HENRY (1): Wordsworth, are you jealous of Aunt Augusta?

WORDSWORTH (3): She wan me quit. She wan for me come bring you, and then she wan me quit. I love your auntie. I wan for to stay with her like the song say: 'Abide with me;

fast falls the eventide; the darkness deepens: oh with me abide…'

HENRY (1): Wherever did you learn that hymn, Wordsworth?

WORDSWORTH (3): We allays sang that in St George's cathedral in Freetown. Fast falls the eventide. Plenty sad songs like that we sang there, an they all mak me think now of my bebi gel.

HENRY (1): Who is this man she's with, Wordsworth?

WORDSWORTH (3): I won spik his name. My tongue burn up if I spik his name.

Ship's hooter.

SIGN – ASUNCION, PARAGUAY

HENRY (3): When I went up on deck after breakfast we were already approaching Asuncion.

HENRY (1): Half-ruined huts stood at the very edge of the cliff and naked children with the pot-bellies of malnutrition stared down on us.

HENRY (2): Above the huts, like a medieval castle dominating some wretched village of mud and wattle, stood the great white bastions of Shell Petroleum.

O'TOOLE (2): Can I be of any help? Give you a lift or anything?

HENRY (1): Thank you very much, but I think I shall be met.

O'TOOLE (2): If you want any help at any time… You'll find me at the embassy. They call me a second secretary. It's convenient.

HENRY (1): You're very kind.

O'TOOLE (2): You are a friend of Lucinda.

HENRY (1): When at last the formalities were over, I stood beside my luggage on the corner of a long colonnaded street. In spite of the dirt and fumes of old cars the air was sweet with orange blossom.

Taxi sounds. WORDSWORTH whistles.

I turned to see Wordsworth in a taxi.

WORDSWORTH (3): We drive around a bit. Ar want to see if they lef us alone.

HENRY (1): Suppose we're not left alone, what do we do?

WORDSWORTH (3): We tak bloody good care. We stop here.

Taxi stops. Cicadas, jungle night.

HENRY (1): It was an enormous house with a great untidy lawn which ended in a small wood of banana, lemon, grapefruit, lapacho. It's a millionaire's house.

WORDSWORTH (3): You just wait.

HENRY (2): The iron gates were rusty and padlocked, draped with barbed wire. We went up one flight of stone steps and into the hall of the house.

WORDSWORTH (3): Hi! Hi! Mr Pullen be here.

HENRY (2): Paved with cracked marble, the big hall was unfurnished. The windows had been shuttered and the only light came from a bare globe in the ceiling.

HENRY (1): There was no chair, no table, no sofa, no pictures.

HENRY (2): A flight of pink marble stairs rose to the first floor, at the top of them my aunt appeared.

AUNT AUGUSTA (1): Why, Henry, you are welcome home. I am so sorry that Mr Visconti is not here to greet you. I had expected him yesterday.

HENRY (2): Mr Visconti?

AUNT AUGUSTA (1): Yes, Mr Visconti. We are happily reunited. Did you bring the picture safely?

WORDSWORTH (3): Ar got it.

AUNT AUGUSTA (1): Mr Visconti will be relieved. He was afraid of the customs. You look well, Henry. Come, let me show you your room.

HENRY (2): The room contained a bed and a chair and nothing else.

AUNT AUGUSTA (1): The furniture will be arriving any day now.

HENRY (2): I opened another door and saw a room which was empty except for two mattresses laid together on the floor.

AUNT AUGUSTA (1): When Mr Visconti is back, we plan to give you a party. A house like this is made for parties.

HENRY (2): You will need a little furniture first, Aunt Augusta.

AUNT AUGUSTA (1): That goes without saying. Mr Visconti has taken to an Argentine passport and he is known here as Mr Izquierdo.

HENRY (2): I am not altogether surprised. I told her how the detectives acting for Interpol had searched her flat.

AUNT AUGUSTA (1): It's absurd of them to treat Mr Visconti like a common war criminal. There are lots of such men hidden here. Martin Bormann is just across the border in Brazil and the unspeakable Dr Mengele of Auschwitz is said to be with the army near the Bolivian border. Why doesn't Interpol do anything about them? Mr Visconti was always very kind to Jews. Why should he be chased out of the Argentine where he was doing quite well in the antique business? Mr Visconti had sold a picture to a private purchaser and this American, who claimed to be a representative of the Metropolitan Museum, said the picture had been looted.

HENRY (2): Was the man's name O'Toole by any chance?

AUNT AUGUSTA (1): It was.

HENRY (2): He's here in Asuncion now. He was with me on the boat and he told me he was doing social research.

AUNT AUGUSTA (1): That's quite untrue. Like the Metropolitan Museum. He's in the CIA.

HENRY (2): He's Tooley's father.

AUNT AUGUSTA (1): Tooley?

HENRY (2): The girl on the Orient Express.

AUNT AUGUSTA (1): How very interesting. I wonder if that could be of any use to us. You say he was on the boat with you?

HENRY (2): Yes

AUNT AUGUSTA (1): He may have been following you. Such a fuss about a few pictures.

HENRY (2): Aunt Augusta, I can't help being puzzled. This big house and no furniture... and Wordsworth here with you.

AUNT AUGUSTA (1): I brought him from Paris. I was travelling with rather a lot of ready money – you remember the ingot. A frail old lady like myself needed a bodyguard.

HENRY (2): But where has all your money gone, Aunt Augusta?

AUNT AUGUSTA (1): When I arrived here poor Mr Visconti was in a very low state. All his money had gone on his new passport and bribes to the police. He was sick too, poor fellow.

HENRY (2): So you gave him your money a second time, Aunt Augusta?

AUNT AUGUSTA (1): Of course, what do you expect? He needed it. We bought this house for a song and what was left has been well invested. We have a half share in a very promising enterprise.

HENRY (2): A Dakota by any chance?

AUNT AUGUSTA (1): Mr Visconti will tell you all about it himself.

HENRY (2): Where is he?

AUNT AUGUSTA (1): He meant to be back yesterday. There are always delays in Panama.

Lights change, street noises, marching feet.

HENRY (1): The next day Mr Visconti had not returned. My aunt slept late and I walked around the town…

HENRY (3): Preparations were in progress for some festival.

HENRY (2): Outside the cathedral and the military academy, squads of soldiers goose-stepped. There were pictures of the General everywhere.

Lights change – back to house.

When I returned home I could hear voices sounding hollowly from the empty hall.

AUNT AUGUSTA (1): I am not your bebi gel, Wordsworth, any more. Understand that. I have kept enough money for you to return to Europe…

WORDSWORTH (3): Ar no wan yo money.

AUNT AUGUSTA (1): You've taken plenty of it in the past.

WORDSWORTH (3): Ar tak yo money them times because you lov me, you slip with me, you lak jig-jig with Wordsworth. Now you no slip with me, you no lov me, I no wan your damn money.

AUNT AUGUSTA (1): Don't you understand, Wordsworth, all that's finished now I have Mr Visconti back. Mr Visconti wants you to go, and I want what he wants.

WORDSWORTH (3): He be feared of Wordsworth.

AUNT AUGUSTA (1): Dear, dear Wordsworth, it's you who should be afraid. I want you to leave me now – today – don't you understand that?

WORDSWORTH (3): Okay, ar go. You ask me an ar go. Ar no feared of that man. But you no slip with me no more an ar go. Goodbye, Mr Pullen. Man, darkness deepens, sure thing, sure thing, she no abide with me.

HENRY (?): He ignored my proffered fifty dollar note and went off down the garden.

HENRY (3): You must love Mr Visconti a great deal. Is he worth it?

AUNT AUGUSTA (1): To me he is. I like men who are untouchable. I've never wanted a man who needed me, Henry. Your father was pretty untouchable too.

HENRY (3): You are not untouchable, Aunt Augusta.

AUNT AUGUSTA (1): That's why I need a man who is. (*Fade to night.*) I don't know what's keeping him…

HENRY (1): We were talking later that evening. Mr Visconti had still not appeared and my aunt was anxious.

HENRY (3): There can't be anything seriously wrong. If there had been an accident you would have heard from the police.

AUNT AUGUSTA (1): My dear, this is Paraguay. I am afraid of the police.

HENRY (3): Then why do you stay here?

AUNT AUGUSTA (1): Mr Visconti hasn't all that much choice.

HENRY (3): Why did you want me to come?

AUNT AUGUSTA (1): You are the only family I have, Henry – and Mr Visconti wants somebody he can trust to keep the books.

HENRY (3): I planned to leave after I had seen you.

AUNT AUGUSTA (1): Leave? Why?

HENRY (3): I was thinking that perhaps it's almost time I settled down.

AUNT AUGUSTA (1): What else have you been doing? For far too long.

HENRY (3): And married I was going to say.

AUNT AUGUSTA (1): You are suffering from loneliness, that's all. You won't be lonely here.

HENRY (3): I really think Miss Keene loves me a little. I get a bit of pleasure from the thought that perhaps I could make her happy.

AUNT AUGUSTA (1): In a year what would you two have to talk about? She would sit over her tatting – I didn't realize that anyone still tatted – and you would read gardening catalogues. Do you know what you'll think about when you can't sleep in your double bed? You will think how every day you are getting a little closer to death. It will stand there as close as the bedroom wall. And you'll become more and more afraid of the wall because nothing can prevent you coming nearer and nearer to it every night.

HENRY (3): You may be right, Aunt Augusta, but isn't it the same everywhere at our age?

AUNT AUGUSTA (1): Not here it isn't. Tomorrow you may be shot in the street by a policeman because you haven't understood Guarani, or a man may knife you because you can't speak Spanish. Next week, when we have our Dakota, perhaps it will crash with you over Argentina. My dear Henry, if you live with us, you won't be edging day by day across to any last wall. The wall will find you of its own accord without your help, and every day you live will seem to you a kind of victory. I only hope the wall hasn't found Mr Visconti. If it has I will have to go out and look for it myself.

SIGN – THE GAOL

HENRY (1): (*In gaol.*) Dear Miss Keene, I have today insulted the ruling party of Paraguay and I'm mixed up with a war criminal wanted by Interpol. For the first offence the maximum penalty is ten years. I am in a small cell ten feet by six, and I have nothing to sleep on but a piece of sacking.

HENRY (2): (*In gaol.*) As it is National Day everyone is expected to wear red, the colour of the ruling party to which the General belongs. My aunt gave me a red scarf which I stuck in my breast pocket. Outside the party headquarters I was questioned and with the heat, the sun and the scent of flowers I was overcome by a fit of sneezing. Without thinking I drew my aunt's red scarf from my pocket and blew my nose. It was most unfortunate. I was knocked to the ground and brought here to the local jail. I kept on saying British
Embassy – but it didn't make much difference. I even said American Embassy Senor O"Toole and I think someone understood.

HENRY (3): (*In gaol.*) I have no idea what is going to happen next, but I confess I am not altogether unhappy. I am too deeply interested.

HENRY (1): I would never really be able to write such a letter to Miss Keene, she would be quite unable to reconcile the writer with the man she had known.

O'TOOLE (2): You seem to be in trouble, Henry.

HENRY (1): Look, O'Toole, you know the ropes here, you might ring up the British Embassy. If I'm to have ten years in prison I'd like a bed and a chair.

O'TOOLE (2): Sure, I can arrange all that. I guess I could arrange your release too – the Chief of Police is a good friend of mine...

HENRY (1): I think my aunt knows him too.

O'TOOLE (2): Don't bank on that. We've had some fresh information about your relative. You seem to be mixed up with pretty shady characters, Henry.

HENRY (1): My aunt's an old lady of seventy-five. I thought suddenly of The Doggies Church, the gold ingot and the establishment behind the Messaggero. I would have certainly called her career shady myself nine months ago. Now there seemed nothing so very wrong in her curriculum vitae, nothing so wrong as thirty years in a bank. I don't see what you can have against her.

O'TOOLE (2): I have persuaded the police to keep her friend Mr Izquierdo out of circulation for a while.

HENRY (1): But my aunt has been expecting him. She'll be mad with worry. Is that part of your urinary research?

O'TOOLE (2): I guess I sort of lied to you, Henry.

HENRY (1): Are you in the CIA like Tooley told me?

O'TOOLE (2): Well… kind of… not exactly. Henry, I want to help you. Any friend of Lucinda can count on me. We can have this whole thing tied up in a few hours. Visconti's not important, not like Mengele or Bormann.

HENRY (1): I thought we were talking about Mr Izquierdo.

O'TOOLE (2): You and I know it's the same man.

HENRY (1): I don't know a thing. I'm simply here on a visit.

O'TOOLE (2): I think there was a good reason why Wordsworth met you in Formosa, Henry. Anyway I'd like to have a word with your aunt.

HENRY (1): Are you offering her some kind of bargain?

O'TOOLE (2): I just want to talk to her, Henry.

HENRY (1): I was feeling very cramped on the sacking, and I saw no reason why not to agree. Some hours later we reached the mansion.

SIGN – THE MANSION

Garden, night.

HENRY (1): As we came through the trees at the bottom of the garden…

A torch beam flashes.

HENRY (3): Are you having the place watched?

O'TOOLE (2): Not me, Henry. Perhaps Mr Visconti employs a bodyguard?

Lights up inside mansion.

HENRY (1): We went up the steps into the house.

AUNT AUGUSTA (1): Where on earth have you been, Henry?

HENRY (3): In prison. Mr O'Toole helped me to get out.

AUNT AUGUSTA (1): I never expected to see Mr O'Toole in my house. Not after what he did to Mr Izquierdo in Argentina. So you are Mr O'Toole.

O'TOOLE (2): Yes, Miss Bertram. I thought it would be a good thing if we could have a friendly talk. I know how anxious you must be about Mr Visconti. I could help to restore him to you.

AUNT AUGUSTA (1): I'm not in the least anxious about Mr Visconti.

O'TOOLE (2): I thought perhaps… that not knowing where he was…

AUNT AUGUSTA (1): I know perfectly well where he is. He's in the lavatory.

HENRY (1): I waited with excited curiosity to meet Mr Visconti. I had an image in my mind's eye of an Italian, tall, dark and lean, as aristocratic as his name. But the man who came through the door was short, bald and fat, and most of his teeth were missing.

VISCONTI (3): To whom do I have the pleasure…

O'TOOLE (2): You are Mr Visconti?

VISCONTI (3): My name is Izquierdo.

O'TOOLE (2): My name's O'Toole.

VISCONTI (3): In that case, pleasure is not the word I ought to use.

O'TOOLE (2): I thought you were safe in jail.

VISCONTI (3): The police and I came to an understanding.

O'TOOLE (2): That's what I've come here for – an understanding.

VISCONTI (3): An understanding is always possible.

HENRY (3): Mr Visconti said as if he was quoting from a well known source, perhaps from Machiavelli.

VISCONTI (3): An understanding is always possible if there are equal advantages on either side.

O'TOOLE (2): I've come here to propose an arrangement, Mr Visconti. Suppose we persuaded Interpol to close the files on you and told the local police we were not interested any more.

VISCONTI (3): It's an interesting proposal. You obviously imagine I have something to offer you in return?

O'TOOLE (2): We are prepared to do a deal.

VISCONTI (3): I'm a businessman. In my time I've had dealings with many governments. Saudi Arabia, Turkey, the Vatican.

O'TOOLE (2): And the Gestapo.

VISCONTI (3): They were not gentlemen. Force of circumstances alone impelled me.

O'TOOLE (2): Unless you deal with us you'll never be able to live in this house of yours. I wouldn't bother about buying the furniture.

VISCONTI (3): The furniture is no longer a problem. My Dakota did not return empty yesterday from Argentina. So many chandeliers for so many cigarettes. The bed was an expensive item.

O'TOOLE (2): I'm offering you security as well as money.

VISCONTI (3). I'm used to being insecure.

O'TOOLE (2): During the last war you were employed in Italy by the Germans to acquire art treasures for the Third Reich. In 1944, you collected from Prince Lampedusa a drawing of great value.

VISCONTI (3): The Prince gave it to me quite voluntarily to present to Field Marshal Goering.

O'TOOLE (2): But the picture never reached the Marshal's Headquarters. I am empowered to offer you ten thousand dollars for the return of the picture, and you have my word that while you stay in Paraguay you will be left in peace.

VISCONTI (3): But what makes you think I still possess such a picture – after twenty-five years.

O'TOOLE (2): We have reason to believe you gave it for safe keeping to an accomplice at that time, and I believe Mr Pulling brought it here when he arrived three days ago.

VISCONTI (3): Fetch me the picture.

Bodyguard gives picture to O'Toole.

O'TOOLE (2): I don't understand. This is a photograph of Freetown harbour. It should have been a drawing by Leonardo da Vinci. I'll have you pulled in again in the morning whatever bribes you pay. The Ambassador himself...

VISCONTI (3): Ten thousand dollars was the agreed price, but I'll accept payment in the local currency if it's more convenient.

O'TOOLE (2): For a photograph of a lot of black women.

VISCONTI (3): If you really want the photograph I would throw it in with the other.

O'TOOLE (2): What other?

VISCONTI (3): The Prince's picture.

He undoes the back of the frame and takes out the Leonardo drawing.

There you are. Is anything wrong?

O'TOOLE (2): I guess I thought it would be a madonna.

VISCONTI (3): Leonardo was not primarily interested in madonnas. He was the chief engineer of the Pope's army. Now this, as you can see, is a device for attacking the walls of a city. A sort of dredge. It grabs out the foundations of a wall and throws the stones up to this catapult which projects them into the city.

O'TOOLE (2): Would it work?

VISCONTI (3): I'm no engineer, but I challenge anyone today to make so beautiful a drawing of a dredge.

O'TOOLE (2): I guess you're right. So this is the real McCoy. We've been looking for this and for you for nearly twenty years.

O'Toole gives Visconti the $10,000 in notes – Visconti gives half to Augusta.

VISCONTI (3): You may keep the frame.

HENRY (1): I went with O'Toole down through the garden to the gate.

Garden, night, cicadas.

There was no sign now of the bodyguard.

O'TOOLE (2): Henry, it goes against the grain to see the US government pay ten thousand dollars for a stolen picture. I got a letter today from Lucinda. She writes about a boyfriend of hers. She says they are hitch-hiking to Goa.

HENRY (1): He's a painter.

O'TOOLE (2): A painter?

HENRY (1): He paints pictures of Heinz soup tins.

O'TOOLE (2): You are joking.

HENRY (1): Leonardo drew a dredge and you paid ten thousand dollars for it.

O'TOOLE (2): I guess I'll never understand art. Where's Goa?

HENRY (1): On the coast of India. Thanks for getting me out of the jail.

O'TOOLE (2): I'm putting your friend Wordsworth on the next boat. Why don't you go with him?

HENRY (1): My family

O'TOOLE (2): Visconti's no relation of yours. He's not your type, Henry.

HENRY (1): My aunt...

O'TOOLE (2): An aunt's not all that close. An aunt's not a mother.

Lights change. Afternoon, garden.

HENRY (2): The next afternoon we were drinking champagne together in the garden, for the house at the moment was impossible. Men were carrying furniture. Other men were up ladders. Electricians were repairing lights and hanging chandeliers. My aunt was very much in charge.

VISCONTI (3): There is nothing more useful we can do Henry than put ourselves in a good humour. My wife is quite happy in the house preparing for her party.

HENRY (1): Your wife?

VISCONTI (3): Yes, I speak prematurely, but last night we decided to marry. Now that the sexual urge is behind us, marriage presents no danger of infidelity or boredom.

HENRY (1): You lived a long time without marriage.

VISCONTI (3): Our life has been what the French call *mouvementé*. Now I can leave a great deal of the burden of work to you. My partner needs watching, but I will look after relations with the police. The Chief of Police is coming tomorrow night. He has a charming daughter by the way. It's a pity you are not a Catholic, he would make a valuable father-in-law.

HENRY (1): You talk as if I were settling here for life. O'Toole wants me to take the boat tomorrow.

VISCONTI (3): But you are one of the family now, Enrico. I feel towards you very like a father.

HENRY (2): Aunt Augusta joined us from the house.

AUNT AUGUSTA (1): I could do with a glass myself. Thank you, Henry. I hope it's not going to rain tomorrow. Everything is a little slow because there are misunderstandings. I find myself looking round for Wordsworth to explain. He had a way of explaining...

VISCONTI (3): I thought we had agreed, dear, that his name was not to be spoken.

AUNT AUGUSTA (1): I know, but it's so absurd to inconvenience ourselves with jealousies at our age.

VISCONTI (3): I like the dead to stay dead.

HENRY (2): What was it that I was delaying? Perhaps the moment when I had finally to decide to catch the boat home, or to pass the border into my aunt's world where I had lived till now as a tourist only.

HENRY (1): The sun shone down on the orange trees, the lemon and the grapefruit.

HENRY (3): The transparent moon was dropping over the horizon.

HENRY (2): 'To hear each other's whispered speech, Eating the lotus day by day.'

Change to interior, night.

HENRY (3): That night, as I was preparing to undress, she came to my room.

AUNT AUGUSTA (1): It's quite comfortable here now, isn't it?

HENRY (2): Very comfortable.

Actors (2) and (3) have photographs.

AUNT AUGUSTA (1): Where did that come from?

HENRY (3): I found it in a book.

AUNT AUGUSTA (1): Your father took it.

HENRY (2). I thought so.

AUNT AUGUSTA (1): It was a very happy day. There weren't many arguments about your future.

HENRY (3). Mine?

AUNT AUGUSTA (1): And you weren't even born. Now again I wish that I could know your future. Are you going to stay with us? You are so evasive.

HENRY (3): It's too late for the boat now.

AUNT AUGUSTA (1): There are planes...

HENRY (2): Exactly, so you see I needn't make up my mind. I can go next week, or the week after.

AUNT AUGUSTA (1): I have always thought that one day we might be together.

HENRY (3): Always, Aunt Augusta? We've known each other for less than a year.

AUNT AUGUSTA (1): Why do you suppose I came to the funeral?

HENRY (2): It was your sister's funeral.

AUNT AUGUSTA (1): Yes, of course, I had forgotten that. What is there in Southwood which draws you back?

HENRY (3): I spoke of my dahlias.

HENRY (2): I spoke of the last evening with Miss Keene and her sad undecided letter from Koffiefontein.

HENRY (1): Of packages of Omo left on the doorstep.

HENRY (3): Of the bells of St John's Church.

HENRY (2): I went over the uneventful story of my life.

HENRY (1): I've been very happy.

HENRY (2): I concluded as though it needed an excuse.

AUNT AUGUSTA (1): My darling boy, all that is over now.

HENRY (3): She said and stroked my forehead.

HENRY (2): As though I were a schoolboy who had run away from school and she was promising me that I would never have to return.

SIGN – PARTY

Music.

HENRY (2): The party was larger than I had conceived possible. The street was lined with cars, among them two armoured ones, for the Chief of Police had arrived bringing with him a very fat and ugly wife and a beautiful daughter called Yolanda.

HENRY (3): The great gates had been flung open: the chandeliers sparkled in the sala.

HENRY (1): On the lawn an ox steamed and crackled. The smell of roasting meat chased away the perfume of orange and jasmine.

O'TOOLE (2): It's a great party. Great. I wish Lucinda could have been here. There's the Dutch Ambassador talking to your aunt. I saw your British Ambassador just now. And the Nicaraguan. I wonder how Mr Visconti corralled the diplomatic corps.

HENRY (1): Have you seen Wordsworth? I half-expected him to turn up as well.

O'TOOLE (2): He'll be on the boat by now. They sail at six. I guess he wouldn't be very welcome here as things are.

VISCONTI (3): Henry, come and meet Yolanda, the daughter of the Chief of Police. Yolanda, this is Senor Pulling.

YOLANDA (2): How do you do.

VISCONTI (3): She speaks English good. You must dance with her.

Party sounds drop.

HENRY (1): They think we should dance.

YOLANDA (2): It does not matter. I have danced enough. I do not care for dancing.

HENRY (1): What do you like?

YOLANDA (2): Poetry. English poetry. I like English poetry very much.
      'Hearts of oak are our ships,
      Hearts of oak are out men.'

And Lord Ullin's Daughter. I cry often when I read Lord Ullin's Daughter.

'One lovely hand outstretched for aid
And one was round her lover.'

HENRY (1): And Tennyson?

YOLANDA (2): Yes, I know Lord Tennyson too.
HENRY (1): 'I said to the rose
The brief night goes
In a babble of revel and wine.'

YOLANDA (2): He is sad also. I like very much sad things.

HENRY (1): How old are you?

YOLANDA (2): Fourteen.

Lights and sound up, Gallop.

HENRY (3): As I skirted the dance-floor I saw my aunt dancing the gallop with the Chief of Police: nothing seemed to tire her.

Fade down, music more distant and establish garden – night, cicadas.

I looked at my watch and saw that it was nearly four. Sunrise was not far off, the lawn was empty, and there were no cars left outside the gates, though I heard the sound of one receding into the distance.

HENRY (1): I felt oddly elated to be alive, and I knew in a moment of decision that I would never see the dahlias again –

HENRY (3): – nor the empty urn –

HENRY (1): – the packet of Omo on the doorstep –

HENRY (2): – or a letter from Miss Keene.

HENRY (1): I walked down towards the little wood of fruit trees nursing my decision close to my heart – I think even then I knew there would be a price to pay for it. I trod on something hard. It was Wordsworth's penknife. I saw the body on the ground and the black face starred with white orange petals.

HENRY (2): There was no life in the black body and my hand was wet from the wound I couldn't see. Poor Wordsworth.

HENRY (3): Poor Wordsworth.

HENRY (1): Poor Wordsworth.

HENRY (3): I thought how his bizarre love for an old woman had taken him from the doors of the Grenada Cinema in Tooting, where he used to stand so proudly in his uniform, to die on the wet grass near the Paraguay river, but I knew that if this was the price he had to pay, he would have paid it gladly.

HENRY (1): Had he drawn it when he first entered the grounds with the intention of attacking Visconti? I preferred to think otherwise – that he had come with the simple purpose of appealing to his love once more before abandoning hope and that when he heard someone move among the trees he had drawn the knife hurriedly in self-defence. I went slowly back towards the house to break the news as gently as I might to Aunt Augusta.

Dance music up – slow waltz.

HENRY (3): I entered the sala where there remained only one couple – my aunt and Mr Visconti. They were dancing a slow waltz, two old people bound in the deep incurable egotism of passion.

HENRY (2): I called out to her as she went by. Aunt Augusta.

HENRY (1): Aunt Augusta.

HENRY (3): Aunt Augusta. But she didn't answer to the name.

HENRY (2): I took a few steps further into the room.

HENRY (3): Mother.

HENRY (1): Mother.

HENRY (2): Mother.

AUNT AUGUSTA turns.

Wordsworth's dead.

AUNT AUGUSTA (1): Yes, dear, all in good time, but can't you see that now I am dancing with Mr Visconti?

Triumphant dance music – daylight returns.

HENRY (3): Mr Visconti has not yet made a fortune, and our import-export business takes more and more of my time.

HENRY (1): We own a complete Dakota now, for our partner was accidentally shot dead by a policeman because he couldn't make himself understood in Guarani.

HENRY (2): And most of my spare time is spent in learning that language. Next year, when she is sixteen, I am to marry the daughter of the Chief of Police, a union which has the approval of Mr Visconti and her parents.

HENRY (3): There is, of course, a considerable difference in our ages, but she is a gentle and obedient child, and often in the warm scented evenings we read Browning together.
HENRY (1): 'God's in his heaven –
     All's right with the world!'

Toast.

SIGN – THE END